Northern Italy 2024, 2025 and Well Beyond

Explore the Best of Venice, Milan, Verona, Bologna, Cinque Terre, Genoa, Lake Garda and The Dolomites, Their Hidden Gems and Enchanting Beauty.

Brandon Rogers

Copyright© Brandon Rogers 2023.

All Rights Reserved.

Table of Contents

WELCOME TO NORTHERN ITALY! _____ 9

AN ITALIAN EXPERIENCE LIKE NO OTHER _____ 11

    A BRIEF HISTORY OF ITALY; FROM THE ROMANS THROUGH THE RENAISSANCE, AND MODERN TIMES _____ 13

    HISTORICAL SITES IN NORTHERN ITALY YOU WOULDN'T WANT TO MISS _____ 18

    12 INTERESTING FACTS ABOUT ITALY _____ 23

    ITALIAN TRADITIONS AND PRACTICES YOU NEED TO BE AWARE OF _____ 31

A FIRST TIMER'S GUIDE TO VISITING ITALY _____ 43

    TOP TIPS FOR TRAVELERS TO ITALY/ KNOW BEFORE YOU GO _____ 45

        WHERE IS ITALY? _____ 45

        GETTING TO ITALY _____ 46

        IS A VISA REQUIRED TO VISIT ITALY? _____ 47

        WHEN IS THE BEST TIME TO VISIT ITALY? _____ 47

        HOW LONG SHOULD I STAY? _____ 48

        SELECTING A PLACE TO GO IN ITALY _____ 49

        TIPS TO SAVE YOU MONEY WHILE VISITING ITALY _____ 49

        ITALY'S TRANSPORTATION SYSTEM AND HOW TO NAVIGATE IT _____ 50

NAVIGATING YOUR WAY AROUND ITALIAN CITIES	*52*
ACCOMODATION OPTIONS IN ITALY	*53*
MONEY AND BUDGET IN ITALY	*53*
HOW MUCH WOULD IT COST TO TRAVEL TO ITALY	*54*
ITALY'S TOURIST TAX	*55*
TIPS FOR TRAVELLING AND STAYING SAFE	*55*
BASIC ITALIAN PHRASES TO REMEMBER	*56*

THE COMPLETE VENICE TRAVEL GUIDE 57

- THE BEST TIME TO GO 58
- BASIC THINGS TO KNOW 59
- HOW TO GET AROUND 59
- WHERE TO STAY IN VENICE 60
- BEST RESTAURANTS 67
- ACTIVITIES TO DO IN VENICE 76
- WHERE TO SHOP 83

THE COMPLETE MILAN TRAVEL GUIDE 91

- BEST TIME TO GO 92
- HOW TO GET AROUND 93

WHERE TO STAY IN MILAN	94
BEST RESTAURANTS	101
ACTIVITIES TO DO IN MILAN	109
BEST PLACES TO SHOP	117

THE COMPLETE VERONA TRAVEL GUIDE — 127

HOW TO GET TO VERONA	128
WHAT TO EXPECT IN VERONA	129
HOW TO GET AROUND	130
WHEN IS THE BEST TO GO TO VERONA?	130
THINGS TO DO IN VERONA	132
WHAT TO EAT IN VERONA	141
WHERE TO STAY IN VERONA	142

THE COMPLETE BOLOGNA TRAVEL GUIDE — 145

HOW TO GET THERE	146
HOW TO GET AROUND	148
WHERE TO EAT	148
WHERE TO GET A DRINK	149
WHERE TO SHOP	151

5 | Northern Italy Travel Guide for 2024, 2025 and well Beyond

TOP ACTIVITIES IN BOLOGNA	152
TOP ACCOMMODATIONS IN BOLOGNA	161
WHICH SEASON IS IDEAL FOR TRAVELING TO BOLOGNA?	162
HOW MANY DAYS WOULD YOU NEED IN BOLOGNA?	163

THE COMPLETE CINQUE TERRE TRAVEL GUIDE — 165

WHAT IS THE CINQUE TERRE AND WHERE IS IT?	168
HOW TO GET TO CINQUE TERRE	170
THE BEST SEASONS TO GO	170
HOW TO NAVIGATE AROUND THE CINQUE TERRE	171
WHERE TO EAT	176
WHERE TO STAY IN CINQUE TERRE	183
MONTEROSSO AL MARE	*185*
VERNAZZA	*187*
MANAROLA	*189*
RIOMAGGIORE	*192*
CORNIGLIA	*194*
HOW LONG SHOULD YOU SPEND IN CINQUE TERRE?	195

THE COMPLETE GENOA TRAVEL GUIDE — 197

WHERE IS GENOA AND HOW TO GET THERE	198
WHAT TO EXPECT IN GENOA	199
WHEN IS THE BEST SEASON TO VISIT GENOA?	200
WHY YOU SHOULD VISIT GENOA	201
TOP ACTIVITIES IN GENOA	203
TOP ACCOMMODATIONS IN GENOA	211
HOW MUCH TIME WILL YOU NEED IN GENOA?	212

THE COMPLETE LAKE GARDA TRAVEL GUIDE — 213

WHERE IS LAKE GARDA LOCATED?	214
BEST TIME TO VISIT LAKE GARDA	214
IS A TRIP TO LAKE GARDA WORTH IT?	215
HOW TO GET THERE	216
TOP AIRPORTS TO ACCESS LAKE GARDA	217
HOW TO GET AROUND	218
TOP ACTIVITIES IN LAKE GARDA	219

BEST HIKES AROUND LAKE GARDA	224
WHERE TO STAY IN LAKE GARDA	225
HOW MANY DAYS SHOULD I SPEND IN LAKE GARDA	228

THE COMPLETE TRAVEL GUIDE FOR VISITING THE DOLOMITES — **229**

SO, WHAT AND WHERE ARE THE DOLOMITES?	230
A BRIEF GEOGRAPHICAL OVERVIEW ON THE DOLOMITES	231
GETTING TO THE DOLOMITES	233
MAIN TOWNS IN THE DOLOMITES REGION	235
HOW TO GET AROUND THE DOLOMITES	238
BEST TIME TO VISIT	240
BEST PLACES TO HIKE IN THE DOLOMITES	241
ACTIVITIES AND ATTRACTIONS IN THE DOLOMITES	243
WHERE TO STAY IN THE DOLOMITES	255
(BEST RESTAURANTS) WHAT AND WHERE TO EAT	258
HOW MUCH DOES IT COST TO VISIT THE DOLOMITES?	261

TRAVEL AND PACKING ESSENTIALS _____ **263**
    WHAT TO PACK FOR YOUR TRIP _____ 264
    WHAT TO PACK: CLOTHING ESSENTIALS _____ 266
    IMPORTANT TIPS FOR PACKING FOR A VACATION IN ITALY _____ 269

THE-ALL-YOU-NEED-TO-KNOW-GUIDE FOR PLANNING THE PERFECT NORTHERN ITALY TRAVEL ITINERARY _____ **273**
    HOW LONG SHOULD MY ITINERARY FOR NORTHERN ITALY BE? _____ 274
    BEST TIME TO VISIT NORTHERN ITALY? _____ 275
    HOW TO GET AROUND / NAVIGATE NORTHERN ITALY? _____ 276
    REQUIRED PAPERWORK FOR A CAR RENTAL IN NORTHERN ITALY _____ 277
    NORTHERN ITALY'S PUBLIC TRANSPORTATION SYSTEM _____ 278
    OVERVIEW OF THE ITINERARY FOR NORTHERN ITALY _____ 279
    A ONE-WEEK ITINERARY FOR NORTHERN ITALY _____ 280
        Day One and Day Two: Milan _____ *280*
        Day Three–Day Five: Dolomites _____ *283*
        Day Six and Seven: Venice _____ *287*
    ITINERARY FOR AN ADDITIONAL WEEK IN NORTHERN ITALY (TWO-WEEK TRAVEL) ___ 293
        Days One to Three: Cinque Terre _____ *294*
        Days Five to Six: Lago Di Garda _____ *298*
        Day Seven: Verona _____ *301*
    ITINERARY FOR NORTHERN ITALY: CLOSING THOUGHTS _____ 303

CONCLUSION + FREE TEN PAGES OF TRAVEL JOURNAL _____ **305**

WELCOME TO NORTHERN ITALY!

Welcome to the magical region of Northern Italy, where the majesty of the natural world, history, and culture are all interwoven at every turn. Take a mesmerizing journey with us across this beautiful region, where tales of Renaissance magnificence whisper from ancient cities, the majestic Alps touch the sky, and the scent of Italian cuisine wafts through the air like a siren's song. From the glitzy fashion streets of Milan to the utterly captivating Dolomite mountain range, our travel guide reveals the secrets of this remarkable region. It covers everything from the romantic canals of Venice to the scenic ambience of Lake Garda. Get ready to fall in love with Northern Italy, where every turn offers a chance for an unforgettable experience, every meal offers a surprise, and every view presents a work of art that must be seen. Get ready for your next amazing journey - and let Northern Italy enchant you!

AN ITALIAN EXPERIENCE LIKE NO OTHER

Northern Italy is a mesmerizing tapestry of landscapes that appear to have been painted by the hands of the gods themselves, nestled in the heart of Europe. This area, which stretches from the majestic snow-capped Alps to the sun-kissed Mediterranean coastlines, is a symphony of natural beauty that entices visitors to go on an unforgettable journey.

From the Lake Garda's majestic, crystalline waters, which mirror the perfection of the heavens above themselves. Alternatively, picture yourself wandering through the enchanted alleys of Venice, where elegant gondolas float over emerald canals and each turn reveals a tale that has been crafted over centuries.

However, Northern Italy offers more than just picture-perfect scenery. It is a vibrant, living museum of history and culture, home to works by Michelangelo, Botticelli, and da Vinci as well as proudly standing Roman ruins that have defied the passage of time.

You'll be transported to a realm where every step is an invitation to appreciate life's sweet, simple pleasures as you travel through the picturesque villages of the Dolomites, the dramatic beaches of the Cinque Terre, or the rich Roman antiquities of Verona.

Your guide to this fascinating region is our Northern Italy Travel Guide. Come along with us as we explore the breathtaking scenery of this area, where each view is a work of art just waiting to be discovered and every moment is an ode to la dolce vita. Get ready to experience awe, inspiration, and an unparalleled love affair with Northern Italy. The journey of a lifetime commences here.

A Brief History of Italy; From the Romans Through the Renaissance, and Modern Times

Two eras of Italian unity are notable in its history: the Roman Empire (27 BCE–476 CE) and the contemporary democratic republic established following World War II. Though there may have been division and upheaval for a millennium and a half between those two eras, that upheaval gave rise to the

Renaissance, which is considered to be the greatest artistic movement in history (c. 1400–1600 CE).

Italy is a country in southwest Europe that is mostly made up of a territory on the continent's core landmass and a boot-shaped peninsula that juts out into the Mediterranean. The country is bounded to the north by Switzerland and Austria, to the east by Slovenia and the Adriatic Sea, to the west by France and the Tyrrhenian Sea, and to the south by the Mediterranean and the Ionian Sea. Islands Sardinia and Sicily are also part of Italy.

The Roman Empire

Peninsular Italy was subjugated by the Italian city of Rome during the sixth and third centuries BCE. Over the following several centuries, this empire grew to rule the Mediterranean and Western Europe. Much of the history of Europe would afterwards be shaped by the Roman Empire, whose influence on society and culture endured long after the military and political intrigues of its rulers.

Italy was the subject of multiple invasions when the Italian region of the Roman Empire deteriorated and "fell" in the fifth century (an event that was not immediately understood to be so catastrophic). The formerly undivided region disintegrated into a number of smaller entities, one of which being the Papal States, which was headed by the pope.

The Renaissance and the Kingdom of Italy

The Renaissance was sparked by the rise of several strong, trade-focused city-states in the eighth and ninth centuries, such as Florence, Venice, and Genoa. Italy and its lesser nations experienced periods of foreign dominance as well. These smaller nations served as the breeding grounds for the Renaissance, which once again profoundly altered Europe. Much of this transformation was caused by rival governments competing with one another to produce works of art and architecture of unparalleled beauty.

Napoleon's short-lived Kingdom of Italy gave rise to a growing voice for independence and unification movements throughout Italy in the 19th century. A tipping point was achieved in 1861, when the Kingdom of Italy was founded, and by 1870, when the Papal nations joined, it had expanded to encompass nearly all of what is now known as Italy. This was made possible by a conflict between Austria and France in 1859, which permitted numerous tiny nations to combine with Piedmont.

Mussolini and Italy in Modern Times

Mussolini was a fascist dictator who subverted the Kingdom of Italy. Despite his initial misgivings about German ruler Adolf Hitler, Mussolini chose to enter Italy into World War II rather than forfeit what he saw as an opportunity to seize territory. That decision proved to be his undoing. Today's Italy is a democratic republic, as it has been since the adoption of the current constitution in 1948. This came after a 1946 referendum in which 12.7 million people voted in favor of overthrowing the former monarchy, against 10.7 million.

Key Rulers

Caesar Julius, around 100–44 BCE

Great general and statesman, Julius Caesar, initiated the process of change that resulted in the development of the Roman Empire by winning a civil war and ascending to the position of sole ruler of the vast Roman territories and lifelong dictator. He is possibly the most well-known ancient Roman, having been slain by rivals.

Garibaldi Giuseppe (1807–1882)

Following his forced exile in South America due to his involvement in an attempted republican revolution, Guiseppi Garibaldi led armies in a number of 19th-century Italian battles. When he and his volunteer army of "Redshirts" took control of Sicily and allowed them to become part of the Kingdom of Italy, they made a significant contribution to the unification of Italy. Despite their disagreement, Garibaldi was given a command in the American Civil War in 1862 by President Abraham Lincoln. Lincoln refused to consent to the early abolition of slavery, therefore that never happened.

Mussolini, Benito (1883–1945)

In 1922, Mussolini became the youngest prime minister in Italian history, rising to prominence with the help of his fascist group, the "Blackshirts." He converted the office into a dictatorship and sided with Hitler's Germany, but when Italy turned against him during World War II, he was forced to leave. He was apprehended and put to death.

Historical Sites in Northern Italy You Wouldn't Want To Miss

Because of its long history, Italy is home to a staggering number of important historical sites. Here are some of the most significant cultural monuments in the nation, arranged from north to south, with both well-known landmarks and lesser-known treasures. They range from Greek and Roman temples to Renaissance churches, and from medieval castles to UNESCO-designated villages.

Santa Maria delle Grazie, Milan: The Last Supper

Though this Renaissance chapel dedicated to Holy Mary of Grace is stunning, the majority of visitors are undoubtedly drawn to the mural that hangs on the wall of the convent refectory. The Duke of Milan, Ludovico il Moro, commissioned Leonardo da Vinci to paint "The Last Supper," which is arguably one of the most well-known paintings in existence. He painted the enormous 15 by 29-foot painting between 1494 and 1497, depicting Jesus and his disciples at the Last Supper just before Jesus revealed that one of them would betray him. The. Purchasing tickets in advance is advised; you may do so here.

Verona's Roman Arena

The picturesque city of Verona in northern Italy is most commonly associated with Shakespeare's Romeo and Juliet, but it also has one of the most remarkable Roman amphitheaters in the nation. Up to 30,000 people might have sat in the large, immaculate arena built 2000 years ago, but damage from an earthquake in 117 has reduced this to 15,000. Even now, events are still held there, most notably a summer opera festival.

Canal Grande, Venice

The Grand Canal, one of the most well-known rivers in the world, most likely traces the path of an ancient river that once fed the Venetian Lagoon. Grand aristocratic residences replaced the cottages and warehouses on stilts that had formerly been on the canal's margin when the Republic of Venice arose via trade. Today, each side of the canal is surrounded by more than 170 structures, the majority of which date from the 13th to the 18th century. There are four bridges that cross the canal, the most famous of which is the beautiful Rialto Bridge.

Venice's St. Mark's Basilica

Although its waterways are a quintessential representation of Venice, the city would be difficult to envision without its fanciful, gilded church. Only since 1807 has it served as the city's cathedral. Originally, it was constructed as the private chapel of the Doge, the rulers of the Republic of Venice, whose palace is located next door. The current basilica was built starting in the early 1060s to replace a church that dates back to the 9th century. The eastern border of the ethereal, café-lined area of the same name is dazzling with its golden mosaics.

The Cinque Terre

Le Cinque Terre, a group of five settlements along the Italian Riviera, is considered one of the country's most picturesque coastal villages. Since they are all recognized as UNESCO World Heritage, they can all be considered landmarks.

Beginning around 100 kilometers south of Genoa, the vibrant buildings of the villages that make up the "Five Lands" cling magnificently to bays along the Mediterranean. The towns are connected by hiking paths and a packed train line, but the best ways to experience their charm are by boat or during the off-season in the spring or fall.

Ravenna's San Vitale Basilica

Frequently eclipsed by its densely populated, network of canals neighbor to the north, Ravenna was, for a while, the capital of the Western Roman Empire. As a result, it was embellished with magnificent churches, the Basilica of San Vitale being the most notable. The interior, which was constructed in the sixth century, is almost entirely covered in mosaics that depict different biblical stories. Eight additional Ravenna structures, including the octagonal basilica, have been inducted into the UNESCO World Heritage list.

12 Interesting Facts About Italy

Not surprisingly, we adore Italy! We all have extensive knowledge of Italy and adore its cuisine, history, way of life, and culture. Given how frequently we discuss Italy, it stands to reason that you are also somewhat interested in the country. We made the decision to learn more interesting facts about Italy by taking a closer look at the nation.

To be honest, we though we knew a good deal about Italy, but after doing some additional research, we were shocked to learn these 18 interesting facts about the country! We also believe that you will be taken aback! Tell us which of the following facts surprised you the most as you continue reading to learn more about this intriguing nation!

1. Italy ranks as the world's fifth most visited nation.

Italy welcomed more than 62 million foreign tourists in 2018. Rome, Florence, Milan, and the Amalfi Coast are a few of the most recognizable towns and cities. The stunning Amalfi coastline and the Trevi Fountain are two of these stunning locations' well-known monuments.

2. Remarkably, a sizable portion of Italy was formerly a part of Ancient Greece.

Before it finally declined, Syracuse, a city in Sicily, was the biggest metropolis in Ancient Greece, even surpassing the size of Athens. Because so many Greeks lived in Sicily and the region at the foot of Italy's boot for such a long period, the Romans formerly referred to this area as "Greater Greece."

It is astounding how remnants of Greek language and culture still exist in some parts of Sicily. The small Girko community speaks a dialect of Greek thought to have originated in the Magna Graecian colonies.

3. The Romans were almost completely wiped out.

Rome's population is estimated to have reached 1.5 million at its height in the first century A.D., but at the time of Rome's destruction in 476 A.D., only 17,000 remained. Approximately 99 percent of the ancient Roman population has vanished, meaning that very few Romans living now can genuinely claim direct ancestry from the city's ancient populace.

4. The oldest university in Europe is located in Italy.

The institution of Bologna is the oldest institution in the world, having been established in 1088 and operating continuously ever since. This is arguably one of the most well-known facts about Italy. More Italian institutions than those in any other nation make up the top 10 oldest universities in the world; Padua, Naples, and Siena are the other three!

5. Italy is among the newest nations in Western Europe.

Even though Italy has one of the longest histories in Europe, it became a nation only in 1861. Italy was a single nation during the Roman era. After then, it split up into a number of independent states, which it stayed until 1861. Because of its long history of individualism, the nation has a remarkably diverse range of cultures today.

6. Cats have rights

It is stated that Romans have such a deep affection for their feline companions that cats are regarded as "a bio-cultural heritage." Killing a cat, whether it was an owned or stray, carries a fine of up to €10,000 and a maximum sentence of three years in jail. About 300,000 cats are thought to live in Rome alone; they are the only inhabitants allowed to roam the ruins at will. In 2011, an Italian cat, whose 94-year-old owner passed away, inherited nearly €10 million, making it the third richest animal in the world (it's amazing that there are animals with greater wealth than this one!). Maria Assunta, the cat's owner, left her "entire estate" to it, to be cared after by a dependable nurse (you might not be surprised to learn that Italian rules prohibit animals from inheriting directly).

7. Rome is older than two millennia.

The Roman Empire began to exist in 27 BC, after Rome was founded in 753 BC. Up until 395 AD, the Empire governed over portions of North Africa and Europe. Up until 1861, Italy was divided into different states following the fall of the Empire. Every year on June 2, Italy celebrates Festa della Repubblica, its national holiday.

8. The last king of Italy ruled for just two months.

Although it possessed a royal dynasty until 1946, Italy was ruled by a dictatorship until 1945. Following World War II, the nation elected to become a republic, and King Umberto II briefly held office from May 9 to June 12, 1946. His days of exile in Portugal came to an end. In recognition of his remarkably brief rule, he is referred to as "the May King" in Italy.

9. The nation endured 20 years of dictatorship.

In 1925, Benito Mussolini imposed a dictatorship that lasted until 1945 in Italy. At his peak, Mussolini was referred to as Il Duce, but he wasn't always a fascist. He actually started out as a radical socialist before becoming prime minister of Italy in 1922. He sided with Germany during World War II, and partisan forces executed him in 1945.

10. Every year, tourists toss €1,000,000 into the Trevi Fountain

You can get back to Rome by tossing a coin into the Trevi. That is the mythology. Every day, visitors throw about €3,000 into the fountain. This comes to about €1,000,000 a year, all of which is given to charitable organizations. Although seeing the Trevi is among the top things to do in Rome, if you're looking to see Rome from a different angle and want to break away from the typical tourist path, consider taking an underground tour. You may also learn where in Rome to venture off the usual tourist path.

11. There are well over 1500 lakes in Italy

Italy is covered in lakes and not just iconic ones like Lake Garda or Lake Como. There are several lesser known beauties too. And you'll find lakes to hike round, lakes for boat trips and quite a few that are wild swimming legends. If you're in Milan, take a tour of Lake Como and Bellagio for the day. Water-lovers will also want to discover the best beaches in Italy.

12. Pasta was consumed by Italians as early as 4BC.

Pasta originated in Italy in 4BC. And what are believed to be the earliest pasta-making tools are also depicted in pre-Roman wall paintings.

ITALIAN TRADITIONS AND PRACTICES YOU NEED TO BE AWARE OF

The world is more fascinating when there are diverse civilizations since there is always something new to discover. Every nation has a certain number of distinctive traditions and practices that set it apart from others. While there may be some practices that nations in the same region share, there will always be some minor variations. This time, we're highlighting the unadulterated splendor of Italian culture.

The main reason Italian culture is well-known is because of its excellent food, which has affected many regions of the world. Beyond their flavorful cuisine, they have many more traditions, even if their food is exquisite and well worth the hype. You will reap great benefits from these habits the next time you become friends with Italians.

1. Planting a cheek kiss

Italians vary from other Europeans in that they follow a unique set of traditions and customs. Shaking hands is not the only way that people greet each other in Italian culture. When people welcome one another, they kiss each other lightly twice, starting with the left cheek. It is important to understand that this is not a kiss in the traditional sense; rather, it is more like the contact of two cheeks without lips.

People's lips continue to create noises in the air, but only their cheeks come into contact with one another. However, you are usually only able to greet somebody this way if you know them too well. It's customary to shake hands rather than give people a peck on the cheek when you first meet them. Most males welcome someone by kissing their cheeks, but only if they are family members. A man might simply give a woman he isn't related to a pat on the back to convey his greetings.

While this custom is deeply ingrained in Italian society, it is also a widely used welcome technique outside. Other European nations that have a tradition of kissing on the cheeks are France and Spain. This is also the way that people in other Arab countries welcome their close friends and family members.

2. Stand up as a sign of honor to Elders

It's a global custom that many mothers continue to instill in their young children: "Respect Your Elderly." Because it is shared, this one is therefore not shocking. The distinction lies in the fact that in Italian customs, honoring the elderly extends beyond simply remaining silent, refraining from using offensive language, or even raising your voice. One of them is to get up when an elderly person walks into the room.

When an elderly person enters a room, those who are seated should show respect by getting up. As it is a gesture of disrespect, it would be preferable if you did not greet the elderly while seated. It would be ideal if you shook hands while standing each time. On the other hand, you ought to wait for the elderly person to enter the room before you do.

3. Take hats off inside

Have you ever watched a movie where the characters go into a restaurant and give the waiter their hats and coats? When you enter someone's home, you should extend the same courtesy to them in Italian culture, but only if they voluntarily give them to you. Wearing a hat indoors is considered disrespectful in Italian society.

By donning a hat, you can shield yourself from the glaring sun, heavy rain, and dirt. As a result, it's imperative that you remove your hat as you enter the house to demonstrate that you think the place is clean, not the other way around. That also applies to entering a church; you never wear the hat inside. It also facilitates eye contact, which is beneficial because it's crucial to look someone in the eye when conversing.

4. Hold doors open

Men have been shown pursuing ladies and holding doors for them in vintage movies. In addition, they allowed the woman to enter the car before them by opening the doors. This is what we refer to be a gentleman, and the younger generations no longer tend to act in this manner. But in Italian tradition, a guy is expected to hold the door open for women and senior citizens.

This can occur even if they are not in a romantic relationship. In Italian culture, being polite to strangers is another quality of a gentleman. A man shouldn't allow a woman race for the door and let it smack her if she is following him when he is leaving. He will be viewed as impolite and disrespectful in this way.

5. Use bread upon completing meals

Pasta is a favorite food of Italians, far more than you may realize. When they complete their meals, sauces and marinara naturally remain, and their food is frequently saturated in them. While there are other cultures where this occurs, the Italian culture has a distinct custom of clearing their plates after meals.

La scarpetta is one of the most well-known Italian traditions. Using this technique, they gather all of the leftover sauce and use bread pieces to mop it up. It's funny how you can tell who's Italian just by looking at their dish. Their tiny bread custom keeps it empty and free of sauces and leftovers most of the time.

6. No surprise visits

It's acceptable to visit family and friends without making a reservation or sending a message in many nations. On the other hand, in Italian society, it is considered impolite to arrive without warning. To avoid upsetting the host and interfering with their plans, you should always inquire if they are available before knocking on their doors.

Social events are usually scheduled to accommodate everyone's schedules and plans. But in Italy, unexpected guests do happen, but they stay in the village. Surprising guests are positively viewed and appreciated in rural communities.

7. Bring a gift along when invited anywhere

It is not customary in Italian culture to simply accept dinner invites and show up. In Italy, showing up at someone's house for lunch or dinner empty-handed is considered impolite. It's customary to honor the hosts who took the effort to tidy their home and prepare a gourmet meal for you by bringing flowers or a box of chocolates.

To express your appreciation for their work, you may also bring a little gift or memento. The next day of the dinner party, flowers must be sent if someone arrives empty-handed. Still, there must only be odd numbers of flowers and they must never be red or yellow.

8. Never yawn with your mouth open

Italian custom dictates that one should cover one's mouth with one's hands when one yawns. Even though it might not really mean anything, the majority of people in Italy perform this as a display of respect. Fascinatingly, when yawning, individuals in the past likewise covered their lips; however, this was because they thought it prevented the spirit from departing from the body.

Other motions that call for concealing your mouth are sneezing and coughing. Nevertheless, this is not specific to Italian culture; rather, it is a global practice that ought to be followed by everyone. This is helpful in stopping the spread of illnesses or diseases, particularly when someone is ill. It got considerably worse when the COVID-19 pandemic struck. But even if you're not sick, it's polite to cover your mouth when you cough or sneeze.

9. Pray just before eating.

All religious communities have a worldwide custom of praying before meals. It's a method to express your gratitude to God for giving you food and health. Italians are regarded as a religious people because the majority of them are Roman Catholics. It follows that saying grace before a meal is fundamental to Italian culture.

Respecting this brief prayer period is crucial when hosting visitors for lunch or supper, regardless of whether they practice a different religion or none at all. Everyone waits until the host or the person seated at the head of the table has finished offering grace when it is time for prayer. The host then says, "Boun appetito," and everyone is free to start eating.

10. Avoid wrapping gifts in dark colors.

Italy places a great deal of importance on gifts. Anyone appreciates getting a beautiful gift, especially if it's something they've needed or desired for a long time. But the manner you express your offering is artistic.

Italians associate colors with deep meanings. Dark colors are not well appreciated, and they notice what color you use to wrap their gifts. When you give an Italian a present wrapped in black or dark purple, they get offended. Always wrap the gifts in colorful, cheerful wrapping paper to symbolize happiness and joy.

11. Use proper sitting etiquette

Italians don't just walk into someone else's home and take a seat somewhere that's free. In Italian culture, there are regulations about sitting that may also apply in other nations. It is customary to wait for the host to seat you during a social event. Do not sit down in front of elders either.

However, if you're hosting, you should never sit down before your guests have had a chance to do so. It's also imperative that, when seated, you avoid extending your arms across the table. When an elderly person is present in a living room, Italians make sure they avoid crossing their legs while seated.

12. There are rules for taking off your shoes

It is customary in the majority of cultures worldwide to remove your shoes before entering someone's home. However, things are a little different in Italian culture. Taking off your shoes in front of the guests is not appropriate. Furthermore, you must wait to remove your shoes until the hosts ask you to. If not, you ought to continue wearing your shoes.

But Italians, on the other hand, never wear shoes inside their homes. They typically swap them out for home slippers as soon as they arrive. In this manner, people keep the bacteria and germs from the streets out of their immaculate homes.

13. Take gifts' price tags off

Numerous retail establishments provide "gift receipts" for a good purpose. These receipts just list the purchase date and do not include the item's cost. Giving a gift with a price tag is considered improper in Italian culture. It could be hurtful to them because it suggests that you're attempting to convey to them that you've invested a lot of money on their present.

In this instance, the opposite is also true. If the gift is inexpensive, some people can feel that you are giving them cheap goods and take offense. Therefore, the gift's price shouldn't be visible to everyone, regardless of how costly it is.

14. No roses in yellow

The Italians love flowers. Sending flowers to someone's home is always a classy gesture, especially following a delightful dinner invitation. Still, a lot depends on the color of the roses. Blossoms of yellow are misinterpreted. Yellow is sometimes associated with jealousy. Therefore, giving someone yellow roses can be disrespectful and interpreted as jealousy.

The most adored colors are always red and white. Red is a symbol of love and passion, which is why red flowers are so common on Valentine's Day. White, on the other hand, represents sensitivity and purity. Therefore, it's crucial to understand that in Italian culture, choosing colors is just as important as choosing flowers.

15. Always take a sip or take a bite before leaving

Italians are well aware of basic table manners, particularly with regard to cuisine. These customs have existed for a long time and are firmly embedded in their roots. Part of Italian culture is the custom of always having to eat or drink something when you visit someone's home.

If you up and depart without partaking of the refreshments the host has served you, you will be perceived as an impolite and lacking in etiquette. One further significant custom in Italian culture is to never get up from the table after dining. In particular, if you are the host, you should wait for someone to finish. But each visitor has to remain at the table until the others have finished eating.

A FIRST TIMER'S GUIDE TO VISITING ITALY

Ahahh, Italy. I'll never get how such a gorgeous country could be both beautiful but be so stressful all at once. One of the world's most romanticized nations, Bella Italia often surprises first-time tourists by offering more than simply gelato, spaghetti, and Vespa rides with men named Paolo. Pickpockets? Swindlers? The all-too-occasional bad drivers so rough that it could make driving seem a nightmare? Unpredictable costs and fees? Unwritten culinary customs that seem more significant than written legislation? And, don't get me wrong; a trip to Italy is indeed, nothing short of a fantastic experience, regardless. However, there are also a number of unexpected traps and cultural shocks that confuse first-time tourists.

Well, not you! Since you are here now. And now, after many years and several visits to (what is, to be honest, one of my favorite places in the world), you're going to get all of my best travel advice for Italy. So, before you travel to Italy, make sure to read this list of crucial must-knows. Equipped with these, you can relish your ideal trip to Italy to the fullest, just as you'd expect from the pictures and see in the movies.

ESSENTIALS FOR ITALIA

- Money: € (euro)

- Spoken: Italian

- Money: Virtually everywhere accepts cards, but keep cash available for modest purchases and tips.

- Visit: (more on this later) Go there in the spring, late summer, or fall.

- Transport: Both cars and trains are available for travel between cities and the countryside.

TOP TIPS FOR TRAVELERS TO ITALY/ KNOW BEFORE YOU GO

WHERE IS ITALY?

Italy is a country in Southern Europe that juts down into the Mediterranean in the shape of a boot. When I was studying geography in school, I always thought this to be really entertaining for some reason. Italy borders France, Switzerland, Austria, and Slovenia to the north and boasts a coastline spanning about 5000 kilometers. While the history of the region around Italy dates back over three millennia, the nation of Italy as we know it now dates back to 1861. Just one of Italy's many fascinating facts.

Rome, the capitol, was established in 753 BC. That it's among the most historically fascinating cities on Earth should come as no surprise! Rome alone is home to several incredible museums and monuments, ranging from the Colosseum to the Vatican. More than any other nation in the world, Italy is home to 58 UNESCO World Heritage Sites! Of the 59 million people living in Italy, slightly more than 4 million are residents of Rome.

GETTING TO ITALY

Most travelers arriving from outside of Europe will probably arrive by air into Italy. Milan and Venice are attractive choices in the north. Rome has a sizable airport, but your best option for traveling even further south is to take a flight into Naples. There are a tonne of possibilities available to you from Europe. Apart from the aforementioned, direct flights are available to Sardinia and Sicily. Trains connect to all neighboring countries and can travel further north than flights to reach ultimate destinations.

IS A VISA REQUIRED TO VISIT ITALY?

Italy is a member of the Schengen region and the European Union. Therefore, for a maximum of 90 days, nationals of numerous nations, including the UK, USA, NZ, Australia, and other EEA states, are able to enter Italy without a visa. But keep in mind that you can only spend up to 90 days out of every 180 days in the Schengen area if you don't have an EU passport.

WHEN IS THE BEST TIME TO VISIT ITALY?

The shoulder season is my favorite time to travel to Italy, however this varies slightly depending on where you are in the nation. Fall, or autumn for my friends in the US, is often my favorite season to visit because there are fewer tourists and the weather is usually pleasant. Nevertheless, it truly depends on your goals for your trip to Italy. The most striking mountains in Italy can be found in the north. Hiking in the summer and skiing in the winter are two excellent uses for them. The Dolomites, however, essentially shut down during shoulder season. Fall travel is one of my best recommendations for anyone visiting Italy because of the views of the orange larch trees in the foreground and the peaks of Tre Cime. It's really awful in the summertime down further south. Due to the excessive heat and crowded beaches, you're more likely to want to stay inside your hotel room than go sightseeing. April through May and September through October are generally my favorite seasons to travel.

HOW LONG SHOULD I STAY?

There are vacations to Italy that are just extended weekends, from what I've seen. There really isn't enough time, unless you reside in Europe and can travel there on short visits frequently, to truly experience one of Italy's stunning cities. Although ten days could give you a greater experience of Italy, I believe that a 14-day schedule is truly the least for a respectable first-time visit. Any stay of fewer than three nights, in my opinion, lessens my appreciation of a location. I don't love having to constantly pack and unpack as I become older. I like to take my time exploring a new city's streets to acquire a sense of it. I simply much prefer slow travel, and I have lists of cultural events, museums, and gourmet destinations in Italy that will last a lifetime. If you have more time, three weeks or longer will allow you to see both the north and the south of Italy, giving you plenty of opportunity to venture off the main road and discover some less-traveled regions!

SELECTING A PLACE TO GO IN ITALY

Selecting where to spend your time is probably the most difficult step in the entire trip planning process for Italy. Here are some of my best recommendations, maybe clearing up some of your doubts! You want to travel to Italy, but why? It's a mix of the hiking, art, history, and gastronomy scenes for me. It could be something else for you. Lover of the arts and history have an abundance of options to choose from since Italy is a country rich in both. We'll be covering a lot of options extensively in this travel guide.

TIPS TO SAVE YOU MONEY WHILE VISITING ITALY

Actually, Italy offers something for practically every budget, albeit there are a few things that will increase the price. Public transportation is reasonably priced, but renting a car can be costly and makes it challenging to see Tuscany or the

Dolomites without one. It's possible, but you'll have to make advance plans and use the bus. This can be especially difficult during the off-season because many bus routes close completely throughout the winter!

You may dine at anything from upscale restaurants with Michelin stars to affordable, fantastic family-run eateries that you only find out about through word of mouth. Local markets or grocery stores can be excellent options for grabbing inexpensive local food on the run to stretch the budget a little bit farther. Of course, there are more possibilities in large cities that suit all budgets, but the true beauty of Italy is found in its little villages.

ITALY'S TRANSPORTATION SYSTEM AND HOW TO NAVIGATE IT

You've probably heard terrifying tales about driving in Italy. A few of these are accurate. I have personally traveled by car via the Dolomites and down to Tuscany on a lengthy journey through Italy and had no issues at all. Although everyone was really well-behaved, I'm sure the people stranded behind me as my van made its way uphill via mountain switchbacks at a speed of approximately 10 km/h weren't too impressed. When another visitor in a massive campervan, on the other hand, refused to back into a passing bay, we sat in the car for ten minutes. Driving around the Amalfi coast was another amazing experience; it seemed as if the bus drivers were in a competition to see who could scare the foreign drivers the most.

In general, you'll be just fine if you're sensible and choose to visit more isolated locations. It would be beneficial for you to review driving in Italy and renting a car there. Most of the time, the roads are kept up nicely and are enjoyable to drive on. That being said, if you're visiting Italian cities that are popular with tourists, driving is not at all necessary. There are trains connecting all points of interest really effectively, and getting around with just public transportation and your own two legs is easy.

It's my personal opinion that you reserve a seat and buy your train tickets in advance. By rail, you may easily explore Europe, save the environment, and have more time to take in the landscape. In Italy, train stations can be found in even the smallest towns. Buses are another option, but they aren't always dependable, especially on longer excursions or in remote locations.

Cheap internal flights are a wonderful choice if you wish to visit the country's north and south in one trip. Italy has hundreds of ferry lines that connect the country's mainland to its islands and other nations. While larger ferries can accommodate vehicles, some are passenger-only and are usually used for day journeys, such the one from Positano to Capri.

NAVIGATING YOUR WAY AROUND ITALIAN CITIES

Italy has excellent public transportation, and the majority of its cities are small and walkable. Buses, trams, and metros are simple to locate and navigate. With tap-and-go capabilities found on most public transportation, you can buy your ticket with a contactless payment option.

ACCOMODATION OPTIONS IN ITALY

Italy offers agriturismo and rifugios in addition to standard hotels, vacation rentals, and hostels. Generally speaking, an agriturismo is a farm offering lodging along with at least one meal. They are located in rural locations like Tuscany and frequently provide activities like cooking workshops. A mountain hut with accommodations, a refugio is the greatest place to stay while trekking in the Alps. A three-course dinner, a bed, a shower, and some of the world's most breathtaking vistas are all included. Look for them in Italy's highlands. Considering how well-liked Italy is as a travel destination, I strongly advise making reservations for your lodging in advance. A visit to an agriturismo is become more and more popular, and reservations can sometimes be made up to a year in advance. Due to their limited capacity, refugios should be reserved as soon as possible at the beginning of the season, which is often in March.

MONEY AND BUDGET IN ITALY

Contactless credit cards are the most convenient way to pay in most places, and Italy has embraced their use. It's also a good idea to carry some euros with you at all times. The best uses for coins are to tip, use the 50¢ coin operated public restrooms, and purchase little products at nearby stores or coffee. Coins are occasionally required to pay for parking if you're driving. All large cities have ATMs, and I usually suggest using a bank's ATM to withdraw cash because you won't likely be hit with outrageous fees that way. Stores in tiny towns might only take cash, depending on the circumstances. Before placing your order, find out if they accept cash only if there isn't a card machine visible!

HOW MUCH WOULD IT COST TO TRAVEL TO ITALY

You may get a general sense of how much you will probably spend each day in Italy based on your type of travel:

- Budget travel: less than €100 per day

- Mid-range travel: Around €90–€250 per day

- Luxury travel: Around €250 and above

Italy is well-known for its flawless €1 espresso. The traditional Italian breakfast of caffè and cornetto used to get you change for €2, but rumors of espresso prices going up could put an end to that! A glass of wine costs about €3, while an Aperol spritz costs €5–€6. A fantastic lunch can be had for less than €20, but it's also possible to spend twice that amount on a classy evening. In Rome, 48 hours of public transportation cost €12.50.

ITALY'S TOURIST TAX

There's a tourist tax in Italy on all lodging. The cost each night varies according on the area and is between €1 and €7. Not surprisingly, the most expensive city is Rome. It is often your responsibility to pay the lodging directly, even if you have pre-paid for your stay. For this, it's a good idea to have cash on hand.

TIPS FOR TRAVELLING AND STAYING SAFE

Italy is generally a secure country, especially when traveling outside of the larger cities. In tourist districts, you can anticipate being harassed by street sellers and restaurant employees who want to get you to come in for a meal. They're no worse than people in any other nation, and you can usually get them to stop them with a stern "no, grazie." In large cities like Rome and Naples, small-time crimes like pickpocketing and bag theft are a sad reality. You'll be alright if you travel with a responsible attitude toward your safety. In Italy, mosquitoes are common from March to November, especially in the southern regions. They are rarely found elsewhere (at altitude) in the north. Another justification for traveling outside of the height of summer! Heat waves are growing more frequent in Europe, and the continent is seeing more extreme weather. Be sure to protect yourself from the sun by wearing a hat, sunglasses, and lots of sunscreen!

BASIC ITALIAN PHRASES TO REMEMBER

We'll be grateful if you can pick up a few of new terms. Before you leave, I suggest installing an offline translation program, like Google Translate, and using it to translate into Italian. The most common and helpful words that you will need as a tourist are usually please, thank you, and hello.

- Please – per favore

- Thanks- Grazie (In exchange, you'll probably hear prego, which translates to "you're welcome")

- Hi there- Ciao

- Farewell – Arrivederci

I hope this chapter has provided you with some useful advice for organizing your first trip to Italy. Cheers to a fantastic time!

THE COMPLETE VENICE TRAVEL GUIDE

Rialto Bridge, gondolas, and canals. Though you believe you know what to anticipate from Venice, no photograph—no matter how well-processed—can compare to the actual city itself. However, it takes more than an afternoon to get to know it. A block or two away, you should be seeing artists creating objects using Renaissance techniques, witnessing sparkling reflections dancing on bridge arches, and marveling at marble-clad structures that are each more fantastical than the next, while day-trippers are swarming from the Rialto to St Mark's Square.

They say that the best part of visiting Venice is getting lost in the city, but no matter how far you walk, you can always find a Titian or Tintoretto inside a few churches. Instead of staying in the city, get lost in the lagoon by taking a vaporetto (ferry) to the beachside Lido, the glass-making island Murano, and, farther out, the islands of Torcello and Burano, which are where Venice had its start 1600 years ago. It would be impossible to fully capture Venice in a lifetime. But it can reach your soul in a matter of days.

The Best Time to Go

Winter is the best time to avoid the crowds because less people are visiting during this season. Though it has a certain romanticism, wintertime Venice isn't the Venice of dreams, with its piercing cold, swirling fog, and frequent wind and rain. The city is packed and steamy in the summer, but it's also the ideal season to visit the lagoon or the Lido beach. With the exception of Easter, spring and fall typically offer the best of all worlds. If you visit between late March and mid-April, you should get fair weather and few crowds. Christmas is usually peaceful, but New Year's is hectic, and

Carnival is crowded from about mid-January until mid-February.

Basic Things to Know

- Money: Euro
- Spoken: Italian
- I'm don't speak any Italian: Non parlo Italiano
- I think I'm lost: Mi sono perso/a
- Central European Time Frame Tempo
- I'd like to: Vorrei
- How much is…: Quanto costa…:
- How does one get to…: Per andare a…:
- Telephone Code: +39

How To Get Around

Trains: There are two main train stations in Venice, Venezia Santa Lucia and Venezia Mestre. Local trains run to the latter station, while only long-distance trains stop at the former.

Buses: The city's public transportation system, known as the vaporetto, runs 20 distinct lines throughout the town. The water buses are available for 75-minute trips along the Grand Canal and are priced at €7.50 each. Additionally, passengers can purchase a €10 Venezia Unica City Pass, which allows them to ride both mainland and certain water buses. Santa Croce's Piazzale Roma is the final stop for buses that arrive from the mainland and nearby airports.

Taxis: At the Piazza San Marco, the train and bus station, and the airport, water taxis are available. If not, reservations must be made ahead of time. Keep in mind that they are pricey, with a minimum fee of €60 ($72). You can go to Piazzale Roma from the airport for a much less money by using a ground taxi (a car).

Car service: Transfers can be arranged by hotels; water taxis are typically used for this.

Gondola: Gondola rides are a must-do when visiting Venice, even though they are more of a picturesque than a practical kind of transportation. Without tips, daytime charges typically range from €80 ($95) to €100 ($120).

Where to Stay In Venice

Hotel Flora

Address: S. Marco, 2283/A, 30124 Venezia VE, Italy

Phone number: +39 041 520 5844

This time capsule of a hotel, owned by the local Romanelli family, is located on the designer drag off Piazza San Marco, at the end of a tiny alleyway. Despite having typical Venetian terrazzo flooring and rooms filled with antiques, Simmons mattresses, Rivolta Carmignani linens, and Ortigia amenities give it an air of luxury. After dark, the retro-style bar is the place to be, although breakfast is served in the little courtyard out back.

Giò & Giò Bed and Breakfast

Address: Calle delle Ostreghe, 2439, 30124 Venezia VE, Italy

Phone number: +39 041 296 0491

Just a short stroll from St Mark's Square, this boutique B&B is next to the Santa Maria del Giglio cathedral and will make you feel like you're walking into your posh friend's house in Venice. Chandeliers dangle from pebble-colored ceilings, antiques coexist with modern white-clad sofas, and the three rooms maintain this blend of the old and the new.

Istituto Canossiano San Trovaso

Address: Fondamenta Eremite, 1323, 30123 Venezia VE, Italy

Phone number: +39 041 240 9711

A unique way to experience Venice is to stay in one of the many B&Bs that are operated by the city's monasteries and convents. Situated in the trendy Dorsoduro neighborhood, the convent-run Istituto Canossiano San Trovaso offers spacious, comfortable rooms housed in a 17th-century building at a significantly lower cost than comparable hotels. There's a shared kitchen, but breakfast is not provided. You don't have to be religious, but you do need to be comfortable with a Madonna and Child hanging above the bed.

Avogaria

Address: Calle Avogaria, 1629, 30100 Venezia VE, Italy

Phone number: +39 041 296 0491

Nestled in a calmer part of Dorsoduro, this five-room B&B will make you feel like a true Venetian. The rooms are modern but playful, with boldly patterned walls, long draperies, and chic bathrooms with mosaic tiles. Selecting a junior suite entitles you to a walled, private garden.

Centurion Palace

Address: Dorsoduro, 173, 30123 Venezia VE, Italy

Phone number: +39 041 34281

Sick of the gaudy stucco and elaborate brocade that permeate the entire town? You'll desire this ultra-modern grande dame with her walls of claret and brown, her modern artwork, and her opulent, gold-leafed bathrooms. Request breakfast or dinner to be served on the terraces that overlook the Grand Canal from the amiable staff.

Palazzo Stern

Address: Dorsoduro, 2792/A, 30123 Venezia VE, Italy

Phone number: +39 041 277 0869

Take the number 1 vaporetto along the Grand Canal and you'll pass this charming, neighborhood-run hotel next to the Ca' Rezzonico stop. It has a wonderful little garden. Belonged to a collector of art from the early 1900s, the fifteenth-century structure is filled with antiquities and prehistoric sculptures. A rooftop hot tub is located above the standard rooms.

Ca' di Dio

Address: Riva Ca' di Dio, 2181, 30122 Venezia VE, Italy

Phone number: +39 06 398 061

This property, which opens in summer 2021, is one of the last to open in the city center of Venice since new hotels are currently prohibited by the authorities. And it's a gem: a stately palazzo with two segregated courtyards for you to get away from the throng and a unique modern decor. Better still? Its roof terrace and front-facing rooms overlook the lagoon, just like those near St Mark's, but it's incredibly quiet because it's just ten minutes' walk up the well-known Riva degli Schiavoni, near the Arsenale vaporetto stop.

Danieli

Address: Riva degli Schiavoni, 4196, 30122 Venezia VE, Italy

Phone number: +39 041 522 6480

This is the quintessential Venetian grande dame—the old residence of a doge from the fourteenth century, with two more contemporary additions. Remain seated in the bar, which was the ancient doge's atrium and features a beautiful coffered ceiling and Corinthian columns. At Terrazza Danieli, enjoy a meal on the rooftop with a view of the lagoon. Optionally, ascend the striking staircase reminiscent of Escher's work to reach the chambers. A select handful feature original painted ceilings, while others were created by Jacques Garcia and pointed directly towards the lagoon.

Hotel Santa Chiara

Address: Santa Croce, 548, 30135 Venezia VE, Italy

Phone number: +39 041 520 6955

If you're only visiting for a short while, it's easier to take the bus from the airport and drop off your belongings at the terminal rather than navigating crowded ferries and hauling your baggage across numerous bridges. The fantastic, contemporary rooms in this charming, locally owned hotel, which is part old convent and part ultra-modern building, some of which overlook the Grand Canal. San Polo and Dorsoduro are both ten minutes' walk away, and charming Santa Croce is right outside the door.

Cima Rosa

Address: Calle Dandolo o Civran, 1958, 30135 Venezia VE, Italy

Phone number: +39 041 863 3022

If the five rooms, three of which have views of the Grand Canal, and the serene courtyard aren't enough to make this a delightful B&B, what about the decor? Greys, pale blues, and eau de nils are the colors of the lagoon, not the classic Venetian grandeur. In the living room, where canal reflections dance on the ceiling, breakfast is served.

Venissa

Address: Fondamenta di Santa Caterina, 3, 30142 Venezia VE, Italy

Phone number: +39 041 527 2281

You desire luxury yet you also want to avoid the crowds. This chic restaurant with rooms that has received a Michelin star is the place to be. This place transports you back to nature with its canalside location on the peaceful island of Mazzorbo and its expansive vineyard at the rear. Burano's multicolored villas are located just across the bridge at the end of the garden.

Best Restaurants

Quadri

Address: P.za San Marco, 12130124 Venezia VE, Italy

Phone number: +39 041 522 2105

In St. Mark's Square throughout the day, Quadri is well-known for its outdoor tables and in-house orchestra that serenades patrons. But at night, this iconic Venice establishment—which has hosted everyone from Brad Pitt to Lord Byron—opens its upstairs Michelin-starred restaurant. Put aside the cuisine, which is fresh from the Rialto market, and the Philippe Starck-designed accommodation; instead, concentrate on the unrivaled view of the well-known square from a covert location. Bookings are advised.

Trattoria Al Gatto Nero

Address: Via Giudecca, 88, 30142 Venezia VE, Italy

Phone number: +39 041 730 120

It's worth taking the 40-minute vaporetto ride to Burano only to stop at Trattoria Al Gatto Nero. Serving the freshest fish that the island's boats net each morning, this delightful establishment is well-known throughout the lagoon. You may rely on Maitre d'Massimiliano to direct you to the freshest fish of the day, and on Ruggero and Lucia, his parents, to prepare it to absolute perfection. Bookings are advised.

La Zucca

Address: S. Croce, 1762, 30135 Venezia VE, Italy

Phone number: +39 041 524 1570

It's difficult to live in Venice if you don't like fish. Regardless of your dietary preferences, the wonderful veggie-heavy menu of La Zucca ("The Pumpkin") will not disappoint. Fill up on the creative sides, such as onions stewed in prosecco or zucca in a sweet-and-sour marinade of onions, pine nuts, and currants. It's advised to make reservations; reserve a table outside along the canal.

Antica Sacrestia

Address: Calle de la Corona, 4463, 30122 Venezia VE, Italy

Phone number: +39 041 523 0749

Despite its convenient location in the touristy lanes behind St Mark's Square, the restaurant's genial proprietor, Pino, is a multigenerational Venetian who brings the best of the lagoon to the table. Take a risk and try something different from pasta, like gratin scallops and mussels, or whatever was in that day.

El Refolo

Address: C. Giazzo, 1580, 30122 Venezia VE, Italy

No phone number

A traditional yet contemporary spot for cicchetti, or Venetian bar bites, the eatery combines excellent regional wines with the freshest Italian ingredients, packing sandwiches and small bread rolls full of anything from grilled eggplant and capocollo to zucchini and cavolo nero frittata. The locals love it, and it's a great place to stop for lunch.

Venissa

Address: Fondamenta di Santa Caterina, 3, 30142 Venezia VE, Italy

Phone number: +39 041 527 2281

Farming has always been a prominent feature of Mazzorbo, an island in a lagoon close to Burano. The Bisol family, local prosecco tycoons, have raised the bar by replanting an old vineyard, creating a vegetable garden, and launching a Michelin-starred restaurant and trattoria (same cuisine, cheaper costs). There's creative lagoon-style cuisine on the menu, plus a little hotel upstairs if you wish to extend your stay. Bookings are advised.

Ae Bricoe

Address: Fondamenta dei Ormesini, 2684, 30121 Venezia VE, Italy

No phone number

Run by siblings Federica, Stefania, and Davide Michielan, this little bar on Cannaregio's main drinking strip is the ideal location to try the renowned Venetian tramezzini, which are sandwiches loaded to the gills. Snag a table by the canal and sample the family friend's herb-roasted meat, known as porchetta.

Locanda Cipriani

Address: Piazza Santa Fosca, 29, 30142 Torcello VE, Italy

Phone number: +39 041 730 150

From Ernest Hemingway, who spent a month there, to Nancy Mitford, this fabled restaurant with apartments on sleepy

Torcello island has won over hearts. You're here for the amazing atmosphere, but the food, which is Michelin-starred, is obtained from all over the lagoon. Set up a table in the garden under the pergola, with the two Byzantine churches of Torcello rising majestically behind the roses. Bookings are advised.

Osteria Ae Botti

Address: Giudecca, 609, 30133 Venezia VE, Italy

Phone number: +39 041 724 1086

The best sunsets in Venice may be seen on Giudecca Island, where the sun sets over the city and casts shadows across the sea. The sun sets like a massive gobstopper here. With tables spread out along the coastline and the Giudecca Canal lapping at visitors' feet, this charming, casual café is the perfect spot to take it all in. You may choose between the restaurant and the pizzeria because the main reason you're here is the view. Bookings are advised.

Ristorante Riviera

Address: Fondamenta Zattere Al Ponte Lungo, 1473, 30123 Venezia VE, Italy

Phone number: +39 041 522 7621

Scoop up a table outside of this Michelin-starred eatery with a view of the Giudecca Canal on the always bright Zattere shoreline. Eat your heart out with the 12-course "Big Market" tasting menu to experience the finest of what the area has to offer, including beef carpaccio, Asiago cheeses, and lagoon-grown fish. The cuisine is ardently local but forward-thinking. Bookings are advised.

Frary's

Address: Fondamenta Frari, 2558, 30125 Venezia VE, Italy

Phone number: +39 041 720 050

Choose a table by the canal at this charming, informal eatery for a short meal by the Frari church. This is your break from

Italian cuisine if you're tired of it; Mediterranean cuisine includes delicacies from Greece to Iran. Excellent Persian chicken, walnut, and pomegranate dish served over rice is called fesenjoon.

Didovich

Address: Campo Santa Marina, 5908, 30122 Venezia VE, Italy

Phone number: +39 041 523 0017

Have no lunch break? Visit one of the storied pasticcerie, or cake shops, in Venice by going here. In addition to pastries, they also provide sandwiches and regional cuisine, such as radicchio lasagne, which is prepared in a restaurant and supplied in a matter of minutes.

Osteria Da Moro

Address: Fondamenta Sant'Eufemia, 658, 30133 Venezia VE, Italy

Phone number: +39 041 099 5884

You'll not need dinner if you stuff yourself with cicchetti here. You may create your own feast, complete with fish-laced crostini and small meatballs, and enjoy a bottle of wine on the outside tables while watching the breathtaking Giudecca sunsets. Also, the pricing are quite good.

Ai Garzoti

Address: o dei Garzoti, Fondamenta Rio Marin, 890, 30135 Venezia VE, Italy

Phone number: +39 041 716 636

Ai Garzoti's incredibly crisp pizzas make you forget that pizza is a relatively new dish in Venice. Try an unconventional topping like nduja and peppers, or their creative salads if you'd want something lighter. The restaurant's menu is complete as well.

Harry's Dolci

Address: Fondamenta S. Biagio, 773, 30133 Venezia VE, Italy

Phone: +39 041 522 4844

A trip to Venice would not be complete without indulging in a Bellini cocktail, which is a delightful blend of prosecco and peaches. Rather than going to Harry's Bar, the original location, take the vaporetto to Giudecca, where Harry's Dolci, the sister restaurant, is located. The Cipriani food and Bellinis remain the same, but the outdoor tables offer breathtaking views of the water.

Activities to Do In Venice
Grand Canal

The Grand Canal's winding waterbus (vaporetto) lines serve as magnificent cruises as well. At Piazzale Roma or the station, take the number 1 and squirm your way past palaces covered in marble, each more elaborate than the last, as you sail beneath the Rialto Bridge, past St Mark's Square and the Doge's Palace, and get out at San Zaccaria.

Piazza San Marco

Most people simply travel to Venice to see the magnificent St. Mark's Square, which is located by the water. Take a stroll down the Riva degli Schiavoni shoreline for those iconic views of the lagoon, visit the Basilica di San Marco, the church completely decorated in shimmering gold mosaics, and have coffee in one of the chic outdoor cafes (we suggest Quadri).

Palazzo Ducale

Address: P.za San Marco, 1, 30124 Venezia VE, Italy

Phone number: +39 041 271 5911

This magnificent palace, which once served as the seat of government for the Venetian Republic, overlooks the waterfront and features a remarkable collection of magnificent buildings and works of art, including the well-known Bridge of Sighs. You can tour the jails and other areas not normally accessible to the public by taking the Secret Itineraries Tour, after which you are free to spend the remainder of your time on your own.

San Giorgio Maggiore

Address: Isola di San Giorgio Maggiore

After seeing the Tintorettos in the large church below, ascend the belltower of this island monastery via the elevator. Enjoy breathtaking views of Venice from this location; visit at dusk to witness the lagoon becoming pink beneath your feet.

Querini Stampalia Museum

Address: Campo Santa Maria Formosa, 5252, 30122 Venezia VE, Italy

Phone number: +39 041 271 1411

Not enough time for Venice's one museum? Choose this one—a former nobleman's home with an upstairs filled with pieces by artists like as Tiepolo, Bellini, and Pietro Longhi—and a ground-floor wing and garden created by 20th-century architect Carlo Scarpa, where the canal is encouraged to lap against channels that have been carefully made.

Burano and Torcello

To reach these two islands, take a 40-minute boat ride (vaporetto) outside of Venice. The semi-deserted hamlet of Torcello, where Venice originated, is renowned for its Byzantine mosaics in the basilica of Santa Maria Assunta, while the fishing village of Burano, with its multicolored cottages, is an Instagrammers' dream come true. Visit the town early or late to explore its true essence.

Northern Lagoon of Venice

Phone number: +39 333 904 3172

Embark on an afternoon excursion with Burano's finest fisherman, Andrea Rossi, who will take you on a tour of the lagoon's lesser-known spots aboard his boat. You pick the schedule, whether it's birdwatching on Torcello or floating through channels that are only a few inches deep.

Teatro La Fenice

Address: Campo S. Fantin, 1965, 30124 Venezia VE, Italy

Phone number: +39 041 786 654

The majority of tourists take a tour of Venice's well-known opera house, which was destroyed by fire in 1996 and then rebuilt. Instead, for a more personal encounter, purchase a ticket for a performance to witness the gold-drizzled stucco up close from your own box and hear the renowned acoustics.

Scuola Grande di San Rocco

Address: San Polo, 3052, 30125 Venezia VE, Italy

Phone number: +39 041 523 4864

Here are some of the best pieces by famous Venetian painter Tintoretto from the 16th century. This building's top level is a work of art in and of itself because it is completely covered in his paintings—yes, even the ceiling.

Acquire a Chorus Pass.

Venice's churches are dynamic museums, often housing original artwork. The Chorus group consists of fifteen of the best; purchase an open-access ticket (valid for a year) to allow you to visit and see Tintoretto in San Polo and Canova's tomb in the Frari church as you stroll around.

Tour of Arts and Crafts

Phone number: +39 349 084 8303

Venice's craftsmen have a long and illustrious history, with numerous crafts traceable back to the medieval era and beyond. Since they are endangered these days, embark on a tour with guide Luisella Romeo, who will introduce you to gold-beaters, mask-makers, and glassblowers.

Stroll about Giudecca

St Mark's and the round Salute church are always in the background as you take in some of the most iconic views of the city on a 20-minute stroll along Giudecca's coastline, the island squaring up against the city center. Along the way, follow the locals into pubs for a spritz; this is one of the least touristic neighborhoods.

Lido

Visit the Lido, the lengthy sandbar off the coast of Venice, if the weather permits, to let off steam from all that culture. This is an amazing deep-sand beach; go west to the unoccupied area, away from the loungers.

Gondola ride

Yes, it might be expensive- but it's definitely worth it since Venice was intended to be viewed from the waters. But instead of renting one on the Grand Canal, head for the smaller waterways where public transportation isn't available and the sound of the boat's propellers is all that can be heard. If you're looking for an off-the-beaten-path journey, start at the train station.

T Fondaco dei Tedeschi rooftop

Phone: +39 041 314 2000 Address: San Marco, 5541, 30124 Venezia VE, Italy

Make your way up to the rooftop of this 16th-century retail store located near the Rialto Bridge. Admire the breathtaking top-to-bottom views of the Grand Canal and the Rialto from this vantage point. Reserve online in advance.

Where to Shop

Rialto Market

Address: Campiello de la Pescaria, 30122 Venezia VE, Italy

Phone number: (no phone)

There has been a waterfront market next to the Rialto Bridge for centuries. But don't just shoot pictures—buying seafood from the lagoon-netted fish market or vegetables from Sant'Erasmo island is part of the experience.

Il Pavone Legatoria Artigianale

Address: Calle Perdon, 1469-1477, 30125 Venezia VE, Italy

Phone numer: +39 041 522 4296

Paolo Pelosin creates marbled paper earrings, scarves, notebooks, pencils, and more. Ask to see his workshop out back, where he creates swirls and blobs using this age-old technique using combs.

Process Collettivo

Address: A, Fondamenta Frari, 2559, 30125 Venezia VE, Italy

Phone number: +39 041 524 3125

Everything on offer, including the washbags, passport holders, and recyclable bags, as well as the amenities and soaps scented with aromatic oils, are created by prisoners in Venice's jails. Employees are always happy to educate you about the shop's partnership with two local non-profits and artist Mark Bradford.

Stefano Morasso

Address: Campo San Cosmo Giudecca 621/A, 30133 Venezia VE, Italy

Phone number: +39 041 564 7224

When you can purchase hand-blown glass created by a Murano master on Giudecca at a lower cost, why brave the throng and souvenir stores on Murano? Stefano creates wonderfully chic, delicate glasses, beakers, and vases; his wife, Nicoletta, creates gorgeous jewelry out of his leftover glass.

Paolo Olbi

Address: 3253/A, 30123 Venezia VE, Italy

Phone: +39 041 523 7655

At Paolo's store, Venetian and Byzantine themes are prominent. The 80-year-old bookbinder uses his hand-printed designs to create notepads, albums, folders, and bookmarks. He has even ventured into creating items covered in leather and cloth.

Marina de Grandis

Address: Calle Larga Giacinto Gallina, 6376, 30121 Venezia VE, Italy

Phone number: +39 041 521 0019

Skip the inexpensive "Made in Italy" leather stores in favor of Marina, a bookbinder and leather worker, hand-sewn items. Pick from her assortment of handbags in rainbow colors or try a leather-bound notepad filled with legendary Fabriano paper.

Ca' Macana

Address: Dorsoduro, 3215, 30123 Venezia VE, Italy

Phone number: +39 041 277 6142

Of course, you'll need a mask to bring back memories of Venice, but make sure it's handmade. Carlos Brassesco creates handmade papier maché masks in both modern and traditional Venetian styles. If you'd want to try your hand at creating a mask, he also offers workshops.

Legatoria Barbieri

Address: Via Giudecca, 283, 30133 Venezia VE, Italy

Phone number: +39 041 528 8493

For ages, Venice has been renowned for its exquisite fabrics. Here, Adriano Barbieri crafts beautiful notebooks, photo frames, and other items using costly fabrics from Fortuny and Rubelli.

Codex Venezia

Address: Fondamenta dei Ormesini, 2778, 30121 Venezia VE, Italy

Phone number: +39 348 546 0257

Nelson Kishi is a graphic designer and artist who shares his workshop with his painter wife, where he creates exquisite, unique line drawings of Venice. Typically written in black and white with a pop of color, they manage to capture the essence of authentic Venice. All of his artwork is available as prints if the originals are too expensive for you.

Banco Lotto n10

Address: Salizada S. Antonin, 3478/A, 30122 Venezia VE, Italy

Phone number: +39 041 522 1439

The women's jail on Giudecca produces handmade summer dresses, silk jackets, and pure woollen coats with a nostalgic vibe. This nonprofit gives inmates life skills training to prepare them for the outside world, and their clothes—many of which are exquisitely crafted from pricey fabrics by Venetian labels like Rubelli and Fortuny—are exquisite.

Dila Venezia

Address: San Polo, Campiello dei Meloni, 1477, 30125 Venezia VE, Italy

This is not your average souvenir store. Beautiful images of Venetian cats are created by artist Laura Bollato and her nephew Sebastiano, who then use the prints to create pencil cases, t-shirts, purses, and calendars.

Collection Muranero

Address: Salizada del Pignater, 3545, 30122 Venezia VE, Italy

Phone nuber: +39 338 450 3099

Moulaye Niang creates one-of-a-kind handcrafted pieces, such as jewelry and glass sculptures, by combining themes from his Senegalese heritage with the glassblowing methods he acquired in Murano. Have a thought in mind? He accepts fee-based work.

Teresa Ballarin Antichità

Address: Sestiere Dorsoduro, 2400, 30123 Venezia VE, Italy

Phone number: +39 347 822 3536

Get your costume jewelry on at this antique store's all-jewelry annexe, and channel your inner Peggy Guggenheim. Unusual Bakelite designs exist; select from classic designs dating back to the early 1900s or fresh interpretations of old designs.

Acqua Marea

Address: Calle S. Pantalon, 3750, 30123 Venezia VE, Italy

Phone number: +39 351 922 1895

Taken out by flooding in the acqua alta? Super-chic gumboots—selected by Martina Ranaldo, who renounced her academic career to outfit Venetians—are a must-have. She wears eco-friendly shoes as well.

Libreria Toletta

Address: Dorsoduro, 1214, 30123 Venezia VE, Italy

Phone number: +39 041 523 2034

Seeking a book to help you reminisce about your trip? Here, in the most beloved bookstore in the city since 1933, you may find it. It contains an extensive collection of English-language guides, novels set in Venice, and recipes for cicchetti.

THE COMPLETE MILAN TRAVEL GUIDE

Of course, Milan is one of the fashion capitals of the world, and it does style unlike many other cities. The Quadrilatero d'Oro, often known as the "Golden Rectangle," is the area surrounding Via Montenapoleone that is home to the world's most renowned brands. Locals stroll around perfectly dressed, while tourists waltz between the stores. This seems like the most contemporary city in Italy at times. The Fondazione Prada, Armani Silos, and Pirelli Hangarbicocca are just a few examples of the modern art galleries that the fashion firms have brought to life in formerly abandoned industrial areas.

And then there's the design scene: in April, Milan Design Week, or Salone del Mobile, brings pop-up shops and galleries to the city, while the Triennale offers a permanent exhibition on Italian design. This city is home to some of Europe's most creative cocktail bars, so even the nightlife is forward-thinking.Milan has a history, of course.

Commencing in 1386, the Duomo is Europe's second largest church, a massive wedding cake of a structure whose complicated design wasn't finished until 1965. One of the best art galleries in Italy is the Brera, which features pieces from the Middle Ages through the 20th century. Of all, this is the city where Leonardo da Vinci lived and worked—he painted the renowned "Last Supper" at the Santa Maria delle Grazie church. The past, the present, and the future are all present in the Porta Garibaldi neighborhood. Milan is one of the most energetic cities.

Best Time to Go

If you're hoping for pleasant temperatures and some sunshine, the ideal times to go are late April and May, or mid-September through October. The city is beautiful because of its calm, yet it is chilly and foggy from November to March.

Because it gets really hot during the summer, many city dwellers choose extended weekends and longer vacations away from home.

How to Get Around

Trains: Milano Centrale is the primary railway station in the nation, along with Termini in Rome. From here, high-speed trains will quickly transport you to cities in northern Italy like Venice, Turin, and Genoa. They will also take you to Rome via Bologna and Florence.

Buses: Although buses are available in Milan, the tram—some of which are from the 1920s—is the classic mode of public transportation. Its metro system is also quite good.

Taxis: You can use the MiT hailing app in addition to the many taxis that have stands at important locations. From the closer Linate station, fares are metered; from Malpensa airport, there's a fixed charge.

Car service: Transfers to and from the airports as well as trips to the lakes may be arranged by most hotels through car service.

Where to Stay In Milan

Galleria Vik

Address: Via Silvio Pellico, 8, 20121 Milano MI, Italy

Phone number: +39 02 8905 8297

You don't get to sleep inside a world famous symbol every day. Inside the Galleria Vittorio Emanuele II, this is the first European version of the upscale South American Vik mini-chain. It's spot on and the setting is unbeatable. The foyer is greeted by a sculpture by Rodin, the hallways are decorated with street art, and the restaurant and rooms face the Galleria (choose one with a balcony if you intend to post it to Instagram).

Antica Locanda dei Mercanti

Address: Via S. Tomaso, 6, 20121 Milano MI, Italy

Phone number: +39 02 4801 4197

This subtle, three-story hotel is housed in an 18th-century palazzo that spans three stories. This used to be an inn for itinerant merchants, but now days it welcomes everyone from hipsters to city dwellers. The furniture in the rooms is voluminous white, and the walls are adorned with modern artwork. For glass walls and terraces, reserve the top level.

Hotel Milano Scala

Address: Via dell'Orso, 7, 20121 Milano MI, Italy

Phone number: +39 02 870 961

Green is also stylish. The Milano Scala, which is situated behind the opera theatre, operates under that premise. In addition to having a living wall, a vegetable garden, and an electric house car that emits no emissions, the hotel is also a sophisticated boutique with blown-up photos from the La Scala archives on the walls of the rooms.

Palazzo Parigi

Address: Corso di Porta Nuova, 1, 20121 Milano MI, Italy

Phone number: +39 02 625 625

Despite having only opened in 2013, this has already made a name for itself as one of Milan's most opulent dames because to its lavish lobby, which features marble-covered banisters, columns, and staircase. The concept is Milan meets Paris, or rather frou-frou feminine meets contemporary macho. Every accommodation has a balcony; choose one with a view of the serene garden.

Mandarin Oriental

Address: Via Andegari, 9, 20121 Milano MI, Italy

Phone number: +39 02 8731 8888

At the Mandarin, location is key; the Brera, La Scala, the Galleria Vittorio Emanuele II, and Via Montenapoleone are all five minutes away. Inside, the feng shui-designed rooms include wide-backed, tall mattresses covered in linens for a Milanese aesthetic, and everything you would expect from a luxury brand, and then more. Take a seat in the humbug-striped, marble-ceilinged bar on a high-backed, curving bench, or enjoy an aperitivo or a classic risotto alla milanese al fresco in the peaceful, hidden courtyard. You'd never believe you're in the heart of the city. Superb urban getaway on a semi-private road with excellent soundproofing.

Four Seasons

Address: Via Gesù, 6/8, 20121 Milano MI, Italy

Phone number: +39 02 77 088

In terms of service, you know what to expect from Four Seasons hotels, but few are as beautiful as this one, located in the midst of the Quadrilatero d'Oro inside a 15th-century convent. The public spaces are adorned with original frescoes, high ceilings, and imposing columns; the chambers are simple yet elegant, and the cloister is surrounded by a picture-perfect garden.

Costanza Milano

Address: Via Lazzaro Spallanzani, 20129 Milano MI, Italy

Phone number: +39 393 564 3501

Which one—the Pastel Home, the Wooden Atelier, or the Greenhouse Loft—will it be? Beautifully decorated, this trio of flats is located northeast of the fashion area, surrounding Porta Venezia. The Wooden Atelier combines a slightly urban, 21st-century look with a 19th-century beamed building; the two-bedroom Pastel Home is a vintage haven; and the light-filled, former garage that used to be the Greenhouse Loft.

Magna Pars Suites

Address: Via Vincenzo Forcella, 20144 Milano MI, Italy

Phone number: +39 02 833 8371

How can a hotel cease to be a hotel? if it also functions as a fragrance. When the Via Tortona district was a center of industry, this was actually a perfume factory. Today, it is a large 28-room hotel with a boutique fragrance situated on the ground floor and encircled by a courtyard full of trees.

The Yard

Address: Piazza Ventiquattro Maggio, 820123 Milano MI, Italy

Phone number: +39 02 894 15901

This hotel is among the trendiest in Milan; in the evenings, residents can be seen queuing up to enter its semi-secret bar without reservations and street-side cult pizza joint. Super-chic interiors go beyond the jumble of antiques and oddities that only hipsters could pull off. Though they are all unique, they all feature something eye-catching, such as polo mallets hanging above the bed.

Hotel nhow Milano

Address: Via Tortona, 35, 20144 Milano MI, Italy

Phone number: +39 02 489 8861

From an industrial hinterland, Via Tortona has evolved into one of the city's most innovative districts. A portion of that can be attributed to the hotel, which draws the design crowd to its avant-garde lobby (imagine orange chandeliers and chairs shaped like rabbits). Rooms with feature walls and clean white furnishings are stylish, though a little boundary pushing.

Best Restaurants

Osteria con Vista

Address: Viale Emilio Alemagna, 6, 20121 Milano MI, Italy

Phone number: +39 02 3664 4340

There's nowhere more romantic for dinner than this "Restaurant with a View" in Parco Sempione, a glass box perched atop the Triennale museum. Enjoy views of the Bosco Verticale, the Castello Sforzesco, and the Duomo spire from the herb-fringed terrace that is cantilevered over the park. Bookings are advised.

Nerino 10 Trattoria

Address: Via Nerino, 10, 20123 Milano MI, Italy

Phone number: +39 02 3983 1019

Though you're here for the a la carte menu and its hallmark dish, turanici al pomodorino fresco in forma di grano, the suits surrounding you are there for the set business lunch. When the waiter pulls out a stovetop cart, sautés baby tomatoes, pasta, and basil leaves in front of you, then presents the dish in a grana padano cheese wheel, you'll gasp. Bookings are advised.

Botanical Club

Address: Via Tortona, 33, 20144 Milano MI, Italy

Contact info: +39 02 3652 3846, +39 02 423 2890, +39 02 2951 9342

You're in for a treat, from the spicy house-distilled gin to the bar that is covered in plants and has a chrome top. However, this is a place where you come for the food as much as the drinks; in the evening, check out the raw fish buffet (try the yellowtail marinated in mezcal and yuzu). Two additional sites exist in the city, but this one, on the hip Via Tortona, is a wonderful spot to meet people after work.

Ceresio 7

Address: Via Ceresio, 7, 20154 Milano MI, Italy

Phone number: +39 02 3103 9221

The diner owned by Dsquared2 founders is located on the rooftop of an ordinary office building. Enjoy handcrafted cocktails beside the swimming pool (which is off-limits) before heading inside the restaurant to dine contemporary takes on Milanese classics at chic red-lacquered tables. Bookings are advised.

Ratanà

Address: Via Gaetano de Castillia, 28, 20124 Milano MI, Italy

Phone number: +39 02 8712 8855

This restored theater is the spot to enjoy the famed risotto Milanese, which is swirled with parmesan, saffron, wine, and butter. You should also get some bone marrow to go with it. Master of the Lombardy classics, Chef Cesare Battisti's business lunch is a local favorite. Bookings are advised.

Marchesi 1824

Address: Via Santa Maria alla Porta, 11/a, 20123 Milano MI, Italy

Contact info: +39 02 862 770, +39 02 9418 1710

So iconic in Milanese culture is this old pasticceria that the Prada Group purchased it. The original, which opened in 1824, is a lovely wood-lined bar on the route to the Last Supper. Not much has changed there. It's fantastic for breakfast, but for lunch you should visit the outlet in the Galleria Emanuele II, above the Prada shop, where you can nosh on delicate tramezzini (sandwiches) and watch the crowds below on the mosaicked floor.

Osteria del Treno

Address: Via S. Gregorio, 46, 20124 Milano MI, Italy

Phone number: +39 02 670 0479

Prior to being the epicenter of fashion, Milan was an industrial hub. This is a glimpse into its history: an osteria close to the Stazione Centrale that was once the lunch stop for railroad employees. Currently, it serves contemporary Lombardy cuisine that are supplied from small farmers as part of the Slow Food movement. Bookings are advised.

La Ravioleria Sarpi

Address: Via Paolo Sarpi, 27, 20154 Milano MI, Italy

Phone number: +39 331 887 0596

Milan boasts possibly the most diverse dining scene in all of Italy. Though it may sound like a pasta shop, Ravioleria Sarpi is actually a part of that; it's a little dumpling place in the heart of the biggest Chinatown in Italy, known locally as "ravioli." Additionally, there's a slow food approach; the excellent meat comes from a nearby butcher.

Fioraio Bianchi Caffé

Address: Via Montebello, 7, 20121 Milano MI, Italy

Phone number: +39 02 2901 4390

It seems unlikely to combine a restaurant and a florist, yet after visiting this place, you'll wonder why no one else has. With an emphasis on seafood, the menu is traditional Milanese. Come for aperitivo instead; the complimentary buffet is excellent and may easily replace supper. Bookings are advised.

Joia

Address: Via Panfilo Castaldi, 18, 20124 Milano MI, Italy

Phone number: +39 02 2952 2124

Enjoy this vegan restaurant while you can because there aren't many vegan restaurants with Michelin stars in the area. Chef and owner Pietro Leeman experiments with the menu, creating many meals with the same item, drawing inspiration from his travels in Asia. If your budget permits, opt for the tasting menus; the 11-course Zenith showcases the essence of the restaurant. Bookings are advised.

Cantine Isola

Address: Via Paolo Sarpi, 30 angolo, Via Arnolfo di Cambio, 1A, 20154 Milano MI, Italy

Phone number: +39 02 33 15 249

It's crucial to remember that this wine bar and store has been operating successfully since 1896. Enjoy the delectable bar food while participating in a make-your-own wine tasting at the counter. Poetry night is held on Tuesdays, and there's a special celebration to mark the opening of a new arrival each month.

Carlo e Camilla in Segheria

Address: Via Giuseppe Meda, 24, 20141 Milano MI, Italy

Phone number: +39 02 837 3963

This could pass for a theatrical set: an old sawmill with its concrete skeleton preserved nearly as-is, but with opulent chandeliers hanging from the ceiling and designer seating arranged around a massive communal table that can accommodate seventy people. At the helm is celebrity chef Carlo Cracco; sample the slow-roasted beef in the Josper oven. Bookings are advised.

Bar Luce

Address: L.go Isarco, 2, 20139 Milano MI, Italy

Phone number: +39 02 5666 2611

Not only is the artwork at the Fondazione Prada worth seeing, but Wes Anderson himself created the on-site café, Bar Luce. His defining style for the setting is a 1950s blend of wallpaper, Liberty-style lighting, and mint green countertops. Select from the numerous gourmet paninis available.

1930

Address: Ripa di Porta Ticinese, 43, 20143 Milano MI, Italy

Phone number: +39 02 3956 2875

This is a truly hidden bar, however it is kept under wraps. The only method to get entry is to receive an invitation from the employees of sister bar MAG Café. The location is completely secret and does not have a password. When you do, you're going to be treated to innovative concoctions that make the ensemble feel like a stage show.

Activities to Do In Milan

Duomo di Milano

Address: P.za del Duomo, 20122 Milano MI, Italy

Phone number: +39 02 361 691

The gothic Duomo in Milan, which is the biggest church in Italy after St. Peter's, took 600 years to build because it was such a massive and complex undertaking. Take the elevator to the rooftop terraces for a closer look at the hundreds of sculptures scattered throughout the structure that resembles a wedding cake, in addition to enjoying some of the best city views.

Brera Gallery

Address: Via Brera, 28, 20121 Milano MI, Italy

Phone: +39 02 72263 230

Alongside the Vatican Museums and the Uffizi Gallery in Florence, this gallery is one of the major attractions in Italy. It is a part of the renowned institution for young artists, which gave the neighborhood its name and featured pieces by Mantegna, Tintoretto, and Raphael.

Teatro alla Scala

Address: Via Filodrammatici, 2, 20121 Milano MI, Italy

Phone number: +39 02 8879 2473

Experience a time travel to one of the most renowned opera houses globally. Get a guided tour of the lavish interiors during the day, or go behind the scenes with a guided tour of the Ansaldo Workshops, where sets and costumes are created.

Cenacolo/Last Supper

Address: Piazza di Santa Maria delle Grazie, 2, 20123 Milano MI, Italy

Phone number: +39 02 9280 0360

This is it, possibly the most well-known single piece of art in Italy: the frescoed "Cenacolo," or "Last Supper," by Leonardo da Vinci on the refectory wall of the Santa Maria delle Grazie cathedral. Forget "The Da Vinci Code" and try to detach yourself from its renown; instead, take some time to absorb the unique ambiance.

Castello Sforzesco

Address: Piazza Castello, 20121 Milano MI, Italy

Phone number: +39 02 8846 3700

Work for the king Ludovico il Moro, whose headquarters was this massive moated fortress in the heart of Milan, brought Leonardo da Vinci to the city. See Leonardo's own frescoes in the Sala delle Asse, which resemble a trompe l'oeil forest.

Navigli nightlife

Although Milan's Navigli, or system of canals, is not Venice, it is a peaceful oasis in the heart of the city. The waterfronts are well-known for their bars, and because they are pedestrianized and have lots of outdoor seating, they are among the greatest locations on Earth for bar crawls. Wander on and select your favorite; we particularly enjoy MAG Café and Rita & Cocktails.

Milano Grand Tour

Phone number: +39 02 3676 5705

Elesta Travel's goal is to take you to some of this hidden beauty's lesser-known attractions while guiding you away from the "Last Supper" and Duomo. Their amazing Milano Grand Tour custom itineraries center on jewelry, leather, art, and artisans; they will design a trip that combines the traditional with the contemporary.

Fondazione Prada

Address: L.go Isarco, 2, 20139 Milano MI, Italy

Phone number: +39 02 5666 2611

After hiring Rem Koolhaas to refurbish an abandoned distillery on the outskirts of the city, Miuccia Prada filled it with pieces from her own collection of modern art. Boundary-pushing temporary exhibitions are held in the main complex, while artwork by artists ranging from Damien Hurst to Jeff Koons is housed in the glass-walled Tower.

Take the Tram

There are few places where you can enjoy public transportation as much as Milan, where the rattling tram network features retro trams from the 1950s onwards and rolling stock that dates back to 1927. The paths circumnavigate the historical center after cutting through it.

Pirelli Hangarbicocca

Address: Via Chiese, 2, 20126 Milano MI, Italy

Phone number: +39 02 6611 1573

The Pirelli tire company owns this stunning modern art installation, which is well worth the 30-minute metro ride. Anselm Kiefer's "Seven Celestial Palaces" are a permanent installation that is unlike anything else in the area. These enormous concrete towers with biblical names were created specifically for the hangar and are part of his incredible rotating installations, which interact with the space itself.

Triennale

Address: Viale Emilio Alemagna, 6, 20121 Milano MI, Italy

Phone number: +39 02 7243 4244

The elegant 1930s structure located in the center of Parco Sempione is currently home to Milan's Triennale, an exhibition of design and art that takes place every three years and covers topics including the interaction between humans and a changing world. A permanent exhibition on the history of Italian design is also located on the ground floor.

Vigna di Leonardo

Address: Corso Magenta, 65, 20123 Milano MI, Italy

Phone number: +39 02 481 6150

Once your visit to the "Last Supper" is over, head over the street to Leonardo's Vineyard, which he received as a gift from the Sforza family while he was creating the renowned mural. Pass through the historic Casa degli Atellani to reach the tranquil garden and, past it, a tiny vineyard with Leonardo's grape, the Malvasia di Candia, which was identified through root DNA analysis.

Bosco Verticale and Piazza Gae Aulenti

Address: Piazza Gae Aulenti, 20124 Milano MI, Italy

The Bosco Verticale, a pair of 'living' apartment towers designed by architect Stefano Boeri and covered with vegetation and trees, is among Milan's most recognizable structures. Located at the center of the ultra-modern Porta Garibaldi area, Piazza Gae Aulenti is a contemporary circular square that is crammed with upscale shops and public art.

Parco Sempione

Address: Piazza Sempione, 20154 Milano MI, Italy

One of Europe's best city parks, it begins at the Castello Sforzesco, runs past the Triennale, and ends with a triumphal arch that almost makes you think you're in Paris. However, this arch is eerily reminiscent of the Roman Colosseum and honors peace rather than bloodshed. Artists such as Arman and Giorgio de Chirico have sculptures there.

Cocktail bar splurge

Europe's most creative cocktail scenes may be found in Milan. The wild Nottingham Forest was the starting point; go on to the brand-themed beverages at Bamboo Bar in the Armani Hotel; visit Tencitt, a "wunderkammer" led by master mixologist Morris Maramaldi; and end up with The Doping Club, the semi-secret bar at The Yard Hotel.

Best Places to Shop
Quadrilatero d'Oro

Address: 20121 Milan, Metropolitan City of Milan, Italy

This, for many, is Milan. Considered the 'Golden Rectangle,' or Quadrilatero d'Oro, is one of the most renowned fashion areas globally. For world-class window shopping, stroll down Montenapoleone (also known as Monte Napoleone) and the streets that flow off of it. A frescoed 18th-century palace houses the Bottega Veneta Home store, which is not to be missed.

Galleria Vittorio Emanuele II

Address: P.za del Duomo, 20123 Milano MI, Italy

A mall that doubles as a historical landmark can only be found in Italy. Designed like a cross, this 19th-century mall features a grand glass canopy, a mosaic floor, numerous sculptures, clever bars, and designer shops. If you're looking to shop, though, the Quadrilatero d'Oro offers a more upscale setting.

Fratelli Bonvini

Address: Via Tagliamento, 1, 20139 Milano MI, Italy

Contact info: +39 02 53 92 151

A group of Milanese, among them the founder of Moleskine, could not bear to see this old printing shop near the Fondazione Prada close to close. Everything is available, including elegant fountain pens, handmade stationery, small-press books, and ancient Olivetti typewriters.

Via Tortona

Location: Via Tortona

was abandoned and is now being revitalized by creatives who are lured to its warehouses. You'll find the odd designer outlet and local designer among the factories-turned-office blocks transformed by the likes of Matteo Thun for companies like Armani; but, visit during Fashion Week or the Salone del Mobile when it turns into a pop-up center.

Il Meneghello

Address: Corso di Porta Ticinese, 53, 20123 Milano MI, Italy

Contact info: +39 339 739 7608

Osvaldo Meneghazzo believes he is the last artisan tarot card manufacturer on the earth, which makes sense considering that the cards are thought to have been created in Milan during the fifteenth century. In addition to making his own cards (the one with a cat motif is especially excellent), he replicates historical Renaissance sets that aristocratic households would commission.

10 Corso Como

Address: Corso Como, 10, 20154 Milano MI, Italy

Contact info: +39 02 2900 2674

Fashion editor Carla Sozzani practically single-handedly turned the Porta Garibaldi neighborhood hip with her store-café-hotel. Enter the lush courtyard and you'll find an entire cultural complex, complete with an exhibition space, bookshop, café, and well-curated ground-floor shop selling designers.

Merzaghi Rino Di Merzaghi Marco

Address: Via dei Piatti, 11, 20123 Milano MI, Italy

Contact info: +39 02 875 455

Since the establishment of goldsmith Rino Merzaghi's business in 1870, the Merzaghi family has carried on his heritage for four generations, dressing the Milanese aristocracy in exquisitely simple yet opulent jewelry. Working from an apartment complex in the city center are siblings Marco and Paola, as well as Marco's son Mauro.

NonostanteMarras

Address: Via Cola di Rienzo, 8, 20144 Milano MI, Italy

Contact info: +39 02 7628 0991

No, you're not missing the address; if you ring the bell on this residential block, you'll be buzzed into a lovely courtyard with flowerbeds and trees. Across from his clothing line is the flagship store of Antonio Marras, where he also sells pottery created in association with Pugliese artists.

Peck

Address: Via Spadari, 9, 20123 Milano MI, Italy

Contact info: +39 02 80 23 161

You will find all the greatest products from Italy in this excellent high-end food store, so make sure to stop by before you head home. You can dine there, but be sure to leave with some delicious rice or flaky biscotti for later.

Cavalli e Nastri

Address: Mora 3 Uomo, Via Gian Giacomo Mora, 12, 20123 Milano MI, Italy

Contact info: +39 02 4945 1174

This iconic shop in the hip Brera neighborhood demonstrates that Milan is about more than simply cutting-edge style. It offers clothing and accessories ranging from the 19th century to the present day, the majority of which are strikingly vivid, vibrant, and more striking than Milan's typical subdued aesthetic.

Rossana Orlandi

Address: Via Matteo Bandello, 14, 20123 Milano MI, Italy

Contact info: +39 02 467 4471

Enter the courtyard covered in vines to find a temple dedicated to design, headed by Rossana Orlandi, who left the fashion world in 2002 to pursue her passion for design. By including them in her curation, she has single-handedly launched the careers of emerging designers; her selection includes anything from deconstructed chandeliers to surreal rugs.

Biffi Boutique

Address: Corso Genova, 6, 20123 Milano MI, Italy

Contact info: +39 02 8311 6052

Forget about shopping around; this iconic boutique has carefully chosen every brand a Milanese fashionista needs for this season. Highlights include all the major labels as well as the incredibly colorful dresses, blouses, and wide-leg pants by Stella Jean and the eco-friendly menswear by Distretto 12 Uomo.

N.H. Sartoria

Address: Via Andrea Appiani, 1, 20121 Milano MI, Italy

Contact info: +39 02 6556 0920

This unique made-to-measure tailor in the middle of the fashion district is where Britain meets Milan. Lighter fabrics and looser fits are typical Puglise styling, while the textiles are imported from Italy and England. Likewise, the N.H.? By "Nobil Homo," it signifies gentleman.

L'Artigiano di Brera

Address: Via Solferino, 1, 20121 Milano MI, Italy

Contact info: +39 02 8058 1910

Purchase rainbow-colored post-pandemic ballerina flats at this charming shoe store on the fashionable Via Solferino. Do you want something a bit more difficult? Made in Italy, the selection includes cozy moccasins, booties, and pumps.

Art Mall Milano

Address: Via Torino, 64, 20123 Milano MI, Italy

Contact info: +39 320 895 5221

Similar to the chair you're seated in? Everything in this bar/gallery is for sale, including the repurposed furniture made by artist Simone Volpin, so you may purchase everything. The bar serves a delicious aperitivo; while sipping your spritz, consider the pieces of art you would like to buy.

THE COMPLETE VERONA TRAVEL GUIDE

Venice, the capital of the Veneto region in northern Italy, frequently eclipses the lovely city of Verona. If tourists give Verona a chance, though, they'll discover a compact, less touristy version of Rome. Additionally, Verona spans the River Adige, which is crossed by a number of exquisite bridges, including Ponte Pietra. The city is home to the magnificent Verona Arena, a Roman amphitheater, as well as numerous quaint piazzas and fountains, breathtakingly gorgeous cathedrals, and numerous ancient sites that date back to the city's founding in 30 AD. When Shakespeare chose to base his well-known play Romeo and Juliet in this charming Italian city in the late 1600s, it contributed to Verona's rise to fame.

Romantics swarm to Juliet's House, one of Verona's most popular attractions, to write messages, snap pictures with her statue, and explore the museum. Verona has established itself as the perfect destination for a romantic getaway, thanks to its many boutique hotels, peaceful green areas, and well-known attractions like Romeo's House and Juliet's Tomb. With this advice, you can make the most of your romantic and delightful vacation to Verona, whether you have one day or more to spend there. This comprehensive reference to Verona, Italy, will assist you in organizing your trip by showcasing all the city's most stunning locations as well as what to see, do, and where to stay.

How to Get To Verona

The Valerio Catullo Airport is another name for the Verona Villafranca Airport. However, they are identical and just use VRN as an airport code. Airlines like EasyJet and Flybe connect Verona Airport to locations throughout Europe; however, if you are traveling from outside of Europe, it may be more economical or convenient to fly into larger international airports like Venice or Milan Airport, as Verona is only an hour's train ride from either city. Since Verona is a small city, you won't need a car when visiting; public transportation is the most convenient way to get around the city.

All of the main towns in Italy, including Verona, are connected by a vast InterCity rail network that offers quick and comfortable train service. For instance, an InterCity train from Rome Termini to Verona Porta Nuova takes under three hours.

What to Expect In Verona

The primary language of Verona is Italian because it is an Italian city, but English speakers won't have much trouble communicating because most young people and service personnel who frequently engage with tourists know the language fluently. Italy is a member of the Schengen region and uses the euro as its currency. If you need cash, there are lots of ATMs in Italy, although most eateries and tourist destinations accept cards. Tipping is customary in Italy, and a generous tip of 10-15% is more than sufficient if there isn't already a service charge included in the bill. Obtaining a Verona Card from a tourist office can also be worthwhile because they are incredibly affordable, costing €20 for 24 hours in Verona and €25 for 48. All of the main tourist destinations, including the Lamberti Tower, the Verona Arena, Juliet's House, and numerous churches, are included in the city pass.

How To Get Around

Verona is a very compact, walkable city with all the major attractions crammed into the city center inside the River Adige, making it simple to get around on foot. You do, however, have a few choices if you would rather or must take private or public transportation in Verona. Excellent bus service is available throughout Verona, especially if your lodging is outside of the city center. It is operated by ATV Verona, and tickets and daily passes are available online. Additionally, meter taxis are available at specific locations across the city, including Piazza Bra and Verona Porta Nuova Station.

If you only have one day in Verona, you may see more of the city by bike than by foot because the city is surprisingly bike-friendly. Piazza Bra, Castelvecchio, and numerous more locations have docking stations for the Verona Bike bike share program.

When Is The Best To Go To Verona?

Similar to the majority of other Mediterranean nations, Verona experiences scorching summers and moderate winters.

May through September are the finest months to visit Verona because of the lovely 25 degree Celsius temperatures throughout this time of year. The summer is the ideal time to visit for amusement because the Verona Arena hosts opera performances in the evenings from June through August. Without a doubt, Verona's lodging costs will correspond with its popularity.

The best months to visit Verona are April through May in the spring and September through October in the fall if you want to go when the weather is nice and there aren't many tourists. Compared to the summer, there is less rain and temperatures are still around 20 degrees Celsius. If you're thinking of taking a different kind of holiday this year, Verona celebrates Christmas like the rest of Europe and has its own Christmas market.

Things To Do In Verona

In 89 BC, Verona was made a Roman colony. More than 2,000 years later, the city's stunning buildings still bear the scars of their Roman past. Verona's architectural wealth was increased during the Middle Ages when its kings oversaw the construction of exquisite churches, palazzos, castles, and bridges. In addition, Verona is located in a fantastic agricultural area of Italy, so you should definitely try the local cuisine and wine. You have a ton of options when deciding what to do in Verona because the city has a lot of bustling commercial streets, piazzas where you can people watch, and parks and gardens to explore! This is our selection of the top activities in Verona to assist you in planning your visit to this lovely city.

Take the Funicular to Piazzale Castel San Pietro

Address: Piazzale Castel S. Pietro, 37129 Verona VR, Italy

Located atop the hill, the Castel San Pietro can be reached on foot or through an ultra-modern motorized funicular. You may get one of the most gorgeous vistas of the city from the top of the hill. If you decide to walk, you should definitely take advantage of the chance to enjoy all the little homes and peaceful streets along the ascent. The castle is closed to the public, although guests are free to take in the views from the square. Nevertheless, from its beginnings as the location of a Roman stronghold to the construction of the current edifice in the 19th century, it has a fascinating history that is well worth knowing about.

See the Roman Forum at Piazza delle Erbe

Address: Piazza Erbe, 46100 Mantova MN, Italy

Visit Piazza delle Erbe, the original location of the Roman Forum, to begin your journey with a little historical context. Situated in the center of Verona's old district, this rectangular square is encircled by stunning medieval structures and towers. A 14th-century fountain with a statue like a Roman is located in the center of it. Originally serving as a hub for the sale of vegetables and handcrafted items, the majority of the kiosks at Piazza delle Erbe today specialize in selling souvenirs to tourists. On one side of the piazza, though, are also little cafes where you may have coffee in the morning or a glass of wine at the end of the day.

Pass beneath an archway to reach Piazza dei Signori.

Address: P.za dei Signori, 37121 Verona VR, Italy

Proceed from Piazza delle Erbe to Piazza dei Signori, a small square encircled by imposing buildings, via the Arco della Costa, an arch with a whale rib suspended from it. A statue of Dante stands in the middle, while other well-known signori are placed atop buildings all around the area. The tower of the

Palazzo del Capitanio, the town hall from the 15th century, the 14th-century Palazzo della Prefettura (formerly the Palazzo del Governo, home of the Scaligeri family), and the 15th-century Loggia del Consiglio are all visible from this square, which once housed the city's public institutions.

Visit the Scaliger Tombs

Address: Via S. Maria Antica, 4, 37121 Verona VR, Italy

Contact info: +39 045 806 2611

Over the course of the 13th and 14th centuries, the Scaliger family, arguably one of the most powerful in Verona's history, governed the city. Consequently, a number of monuments, such as the Scaliger Tombs, were built surrounding Verona. Situated in a courtyard outside the church of Santa Maria Antica, this series of five Gothic funeral monuments honors five different Lords of Verona: Cangrande I, Mastino II, Cansignorio, Alberto II, and Giovanni. Every day of the year, the Scaliger Tombs are open to the public and free to enter; nevertheless, a wall with iron bars separates each tomb from the street to keep visitors from upsetting the deceased lords who lay there.

Climb up the Lamberti Tower.

Address: Via della Costa, 1, 37121 Verona VR, Italy

Contact info: +39 045 927 3027

A wonderful spot to gain a general overview of Verona is Lamberti Tower (Torre dei Lamberti), which is situated close to Palazzo della Ragione, right off Piazza delle Erbe. You can enjoy great views of the city and beyond if you pay to take the elevator most of the way or climb the stairs to the summit. Its medieval bell tower was first constructed in the twelfth century and raised several times before reaching its ultimate height of roughly 275 feet in the year 1436. In 1798, Count Giovanni Sagramoso also replaced the broken clock on the neighboring Torre Gardello with a new one by adding a clock to the tower.

Visit Juliet's balcony and home.

Address: 37121 Verona VR, Italy; Via Cappello

One of Verona's most well-known tourist attractions is the 13th-century Juliet's House, which houses a museum honoring the title character of Shakespeare's "Romeo and Juliet." The museum houses a collection of period furniture that is intended to resemble the furnishings Juliet would have had in her home during that era. The house is a great example of Gothic architecture in the city. Juliet's House, which is situated in a courtyard off Via Capello, is home to a monument of Juliet as well as the well-known balcony where Romeo declared his love for the young Juliet. The bronze statue and balcony are free to view, however there is a nominal charge to enter the museum.

As an alternative, you can also see the residence on Via Arche Scaligere that is linked to Romeo's family. Next door at Osteria al Duca, you could also try some of Verona's traditional dishes, which includes horse or donkey meat.

Check out the Archaeological Museum and Roman Theater.

Address: Rigaste Redentore, 2, 37129 Verona VR, Italy

Contact info: +39 045 800 0360

The Roman Theater and Archaeological Museum is conveniently located from Juliet's House through Ponte Pietra, a charming stone bridge that spans the Adige River. The theater is built into a hill with a view of the river. Roman mosaics, Etruscan and Roman bronze sculptures, and Roman inscriptions may be found in the museum, which is housed in the old Convent of Saint Jerome. In addition, there are summertime outdoor performances in the theater built in the first century AD. Tickets are required to enter each attraction, which is open seven days a week.

Visit the Museum and Castle at Castelvecchio.

Address: Corso Castelvecchio, 2, 37121 Verona VR, Italy

Contact info: +39 045 806 2611

Constructed in the fourteenth century as both a home and a stronghold, Castelvecchio is currently a museum showcasing Veronese medieval culture. The complex of buildings consists of multiple towers, keeps, a brick bridge that spans the river, and a pleasant courtyard that used to be the parade ground is now the museum. The museum has sixteen rooms from the former palace that are adorned with holy artwork, paintings, Renaissance bronze statues, coins, weapons, and armor. Tickets are needed to enter the museum, and tours are offered every day of the year.

Visit Fondazione Arena Di Verona and see the opera.

Address: P.za Bra, 1, 37121 Verona VR, Italy

Contact info: +39 045 800 5151

The Fondazione Arena Di Verona, the largest and most impressive landmark in the city, is the third-largest Roman arena in Italy, behind the Colosseum in Rome and the arena in Capua. Established in the 1st century, the amphitheater can accommodate up to 25,000 attendees and presents a diverse range of musical events, such as prominent opera companies from Verona and the esteemed opera festival, the Festival lirico all'Arena di Verona, which has been held there since 1913. But during the day, when the light is shining brightly on the stage, is the ideal time to explore this Roman arena. Even with the addition of bright orange and red seats to portion of the seating, one can still see the amphitheater's previous appearance when it was utilized for purposes other than attending a play or opera.

Take a Tour of Giardino Giusti

Address: Via Giardino Giusti, 2, 37129 Verona VR, Italy

Contact info: +39 045 803 4029

One of the greatest examples of Italian gardens in the nation, Giardino Giusti is a vast garden created in the Italian Renaissance style and is on the grounds of a sizable castle complex on the eastern banks of the Adige river. This well-known attraction has eight distinct garden parts in addition to a hedge labyrinth and a walking track through a small forested area on the grounds' edge. The Giusti Garden also hosts a number of annual events, such as the Singing Garden, the Festival of Beauty, and revolving exhibitions of modern art.

Spend a Day at Lake Garda

Address: Italy's Lake Garda

Take into consideration going to Lake Garda for the day if you have some free time to see Verona (check out our guide on Lake Garda). Lake Garda, also called Lago di Garda in

Italian, is one of the largest lakes in the country and a well-liked vacation spot for both locals and visitors because of its clear blue waters, comfortable weather, and spotless beaches. The imposing fortification known as Rocca Scaligera, which was formerly owned by the powerful Scaliger family, and Grotte di Catullo, the remnants of a Roman villa that formerly stood on the peninsula, are located near the town of Sirmione, which is situated at the southern end of the lake. Additionally, you may find Vittoriale degli Italiani, the old residence of poet d'Annunzio, in the town of Gardone Riviera on the western shore.

Offer up a prayer at Verona's Duomo

Address: Piazza Vescovado, 37121 Verona VR, Italy

Contact info: +39 045 592813

Known by its other name, the Duomo di Verona, the Romanesque Cathedral is a collection of structures that includes Saint Elena Church, the Canons Cloister, a 12th-century Baptistery, and the remnants of a 4th-century paleo-Christian basilica. The Baptistery features murals from the 13th to the 15th centuries, and the octagonal Romanesque baptismal font was carved from a single block of marble and embellished with Biblical images. The facade of the cathedral is embellished with reliefs from the 12th century, while its interior murals date from the 15th to the 18th century. Seasonally-varying hours apply to the Cathedral Complex's

Sunday through Friday openings, and admission to the amenities requires a ticket. But throughout the year, Sunday religious services offer free admission to the cathedral's interior.

Take a walk through the Piazza Bra area

Address: P.za Bra, Italy's Verona VR

Previously a suburban braida (field), Piazza Bra is a sizable piazza found inside Verona's main entrance gate. On one side of the piazza, close to the neoclassical Palazzo Municipale, is the Roman Arena; on the other, a wide promenade leads through a number of porticoed buildings housing cafes and restaurants. In addition, Piazza Bra has a large garden with a central fountain. This area is perfect for carrying carryout from one of the neighboring restaurants or having a picnic.

What to Eat In Verona

Fish, cheese, wine, and pasta It is well known that Italian food is among the most adored worldwide. However, each Italian region has a distinctive culinary style of its own. Verona is located in the area of Veneto, where pasta is not a common meal. Risotto and other rice and polenta-based foods are far more regionally authentic. Naturally, pasta is still a staple in the area, and a traditional Venetian pasta dish would be bigoli in salsa, or pasta with salted fish.

Prosecco, an Italian sparkling wine, and the renowned Aperitivo beverages Bellini and Aperol Spritz originate from the Veneto area. Aperitivo, which includes tapas as pre-dinner nibbles, is comparable to "happy hour" in other nations. "Cicchetti," or little meat or fish balls, are frequently offered with aperitivo in the Veneto region. Tiramisu, salted cod, and octopus are further examples of traditional Venetian fare.

But don't overlook the gelato! Without a doubt, one of the greatest gelaterias in the city is Gelateria Romana. Some of Verona's greatest gelato has been served at this gelateria since 1947. It's a touch outside of the city center, but well worth it—especially with their unique crema flavor—because of the railway station nearby. A good backup that is conveniently situated in the city center is Gelateria Ponte Pietra.

Where To Stay In Verona

Budget: Verona has fewer hostels than some of the larger Italian towns (Rome, Milan, Venice, etc.), but lodging is often less expensive here. Fortunately, the only hostel you'll need is The Hostello, which is located just east of the city center.

It is a stand-alone hostel with lively, colorful design, complimentary breakfast, and spotless, en suite accommodations. Additionally, they offer a cozy courtyard with plenty of plush furniture where you may easily meet people while visiting Verona.

Mid-range: The Oriana Suites Verona, which is well situated close to the Verona Arena, is a great choice if you're traveling with a family or just want extra space and the ability to prepare your own meals. Each apartment boasts a modern, tidy, and minimalist design, with a spacious living area, kitchen, and in some cases, a balcony. As an alternative, the nearby Hotel Milano & Spa is a fantastic affordable boutique hotel with rooftop hot springs and subtle luxuries.

Luxury: It's not as pricey as you may expect to stay in a romantic, five-star hotel in Verona. The 5-star Il Sogno Di Giulietta Hotel is located in the courtyard of Juliet's House and offers the most amazing suites in a medieval/fantasy design that will make you feel as though you are in Romeo and Juliet's world. The rooms are frequently less than €100 per night. With its lofty ceilings and opulent soft furnishings and decor reminiscent of a palace, the Palazzo Monga Boutique Guesthouse in Verona is the perfect place to enjoy an even more opulent lifestyle. You may even perform cartwheels there if you so choose!

THE COMPLETE BOLOGNA TRAVEL GUIDE

This is one of the most popular cities in Italy for a reason. The center of Bologna looks surprisingly medieval, with red brick, tiled roofs, and balconies extending from Piazza Maggiore. There are enough landmarks for a few days of leisurely exploration here, including the Due Torri, the city's own "leaning towers," numerous little, eccentric museums, and some impressive Gothic and Renaissance buildings. Additionally, because of the university, there's always something going on, whether it's theater, music, or just the liveliest café and bar culture in northern Italy.

"Red Bologna," which originated as a resistance movement against German occupation during World War II, became the intellectual and political center of the Italian Left. As a result, in 1980, fascist organizations targeted Bologna's train station for Italy's worst postwar terrorist attack, which resulted in 84 fatalities. The tragedy is remembered with a jagged, glassed-in gash in the station wall. The city's political inclinations have changed throughout the years, but its reputation as a "leftist" has endured.

How To Get There

The Marconi Express monorail connects the northwest-of-town Marconi airfield to the town center and train station. In the event that you choose to arrive by train, the station may be found in Piazza delle Medaglie d'Oro. 300 meters from the train station is the bus terminal, or autostazione, where all long-distance buses come to an end. Refrain from driving into central Bologna if at all possible. Private vehicles are not allowed in the city center from 7 a.m. to 8 p.m. daily, and there are traffic restrictions throughout the entire town. You can enter the historic center with your automobile if your hotel is located there, but you'll need to let them know in advance.

How To Get Around

Though motorcycles and buses are also useful, walking beneath some of the city's stunning porticoes is the ideal way to experience Bologna. Walks with guides are detailed in the tourist office. Rent and repair bikes at Demetra Social Bike, located at 37 Via Capo di Lucca, close to the bus stop. Buses run quickly and frequently. Tickets can be purchased via ticket machines on board, newsstands, tabacchi, and bus information kiosks. Starting at the train station, the open-top, hop-on-hop-off City redbus takes passengers on a tour of the city.

Where To Eat

Whether you're dining at a pub or making a night of it, you're more likely to have a fantastic bite here than a bad one, in contrast to its tourist-heavy sibling cities. Nestled in the aforementioned Phi Hotel Bologna - Al Cappello Rosso, Osteria del Cappello is a remarkable, tavern-esque venue to top your hit list. The oldest restaurant in the city, it has been serving up the best bolognan dishes to guests since 1345. With only six tables, it's small, so whether you're staying at a hotel or not, make reservations and order the fried tortellini.

Ruggine is technically a bar, but it serves delicious dishes all day long that include modern takes on salads, burgers, and pastas. Located in the heart of the city, this former bicycle repair shop is hidden in a little alleyway. Its rustic décor, which derives from the word "rust," pours out onto the street, taking over the sidewalk with delicious food and amazing cocktails. Ask the staff for recommendations; they will be pleased to discuss the options.

Although Bologna is a meat lover's heaven, there are also excellent vegan options in the city. Botanical Lab Cucina is a sophisticated plant-based restaurant that is surprisingly affordable for its caliber. There's no shortage of Mediterranean fusion dishes or vegan noodles. Whether you are a carnivore or a herbivore, you must try the cheesecakes made with cashews.

Where To Get A Drink

No matter the time of day, Caffe Rubik offers some of the best spots in town for people watching. Its walls are packed with shelves full of cassette tapes, porcelain teapots, and vintage toys, accentuated by the artwork of local artists. It serves strong Italian coffees by day and cocktails by night. The ecological and fair-trade approach is combined with the same all-day laid-back attitude at Cafe de la Paix.

Enter the city's oldest wine tavern, Osteria del Sole, to see Bologna in all its glory. It's a bustling watering establishment with a charmingly simple façade that's popular for graduation parties. Believe us when we say that the graduation festivities at Italian universities are certainly something to watch (you won't soon forget the song). In case you're not too full from your culinary explorations, you can even carry your own food inside.

Senza Nome's deaf or partially hearing bar staff can provide you with sign language advice or flashcards for an interactive night out. However, if you are not very good at communicating, they can all lip read. This high-ceilinged bar serves great food, but if you're more interested in delicious décor, head to Le Stanze, where the sophisticated, fading Renaissance wall and ceiling paintings will astonish you just as much as the cocktails.

Where To Shop

A stylish brogue or other exquisite footwear may be found at the Bologna location of Milanese shoe manufacturer Velasca. Nothing says "I've been to Italy" like a new pair of handcrafted leather shoes. Situated in a converted garage with neon lights and an industrial décor, their shoe vending experience is not your typical shoe store. It's a great place to visit, located around the corner from Piazza Maggiore.

Make a splash and bring home a gorgeous, vacuum-sealed package of tortellini from La Casa del Tortellino, a culinary bar and laboratory that serves freshly created gourmet pasta. Make the stop if you're heading out that way because it's close to the airport but a little ways from the city center.

Bologna, like many college cities, boasts an amazing culture for vintage clothing. Spend some time browsing La Leonarda, Humana Vintage Bologna, and Zero Vintage; they all have great personnel and excellent selections. Maybe you'll find that unique, pre-owned shirt there. Piazza VIII Agosto hosts a robust weekly flea market on Fridays and Saturdays if you're like buying vintage clothing.

Natural sciences have a long history in Bologna, and La Bottega dei Minerali capitalizes on this legacy by offering a unique selection of jewelry along with a stunning assortment of crystals and minerals. It's located just north of Centrale station and is open from 3.30 p.m. in the afternoon after lunch and until 1.30 p.m. in the morning. Perfect as presents or for spoiling oneself.

Top Activities In Bologna

There is much to do in Bologna, including visiting the 16th-century Neptune Fountain and the church of San Petronio, one of Italy's finest examples of a Gothic brick structure. These are the salient features.

Sample the Regional Specialties

Bologna is one of the greatest locations to experience the variety of the Emilia-Romagna region's food, which is among the best in all of Italy. There's so much more to sample than simply spaghetti bolognese. Classic dishes like lasagna and tagliatelle covered in ragu, a slow-cooked meat sauce, as well as handcrafted packed pasta like tortellini, are served at many places. The city is renowned for its mortadella and salami as well. While Bologna has several great restaurants, I Portici, the city's (surprise) only Michelin-star eatery, is a great choice for a special occasion. Make sure to reserve a table.

Immerse yourself in its rich Architecture

Bologna's small medieval core is home to a number of exquisite churches, public buildings, and monuments. Enjoy the city's many porticoed sidewalks, which add to the pleasure of window shopping, while you explore. Santuario di Madonna di San Luca (Sanctuary of the Madonna of San Luca), located on a hill, and Basilica di San Giacomo Maggiore (Basilica of San San Giacomo Maggiore), which combines Baroque and Renaissance architectural elements, are the two must-see churches. Other noteworthy structures are the Archginnasio of Bologna, which served as the main building of the University of Bologna and is now home to the Biblioteca Comunale dell'Archiginnasio (Municipal Library of the Archinnasio) and the Teatro Anatomica (Anatomical

Theater), where researchers used to dissect human corpses for research.

Tour the Main Squares

You may stroll between the stunning central squares of Bologna, such as Piazza Maggiore, which is home to the Archaeological Museum, the Palazzo dei Notai, and the Gothic Basilica of San Petronio. The medieval civic buildings encircle the elaborate 16th-century fountain in the heart of Piazza del Nettuno. Don't forget to explore the Salaborsa Library's inside.

Sample New Flavors Along Via Clavature

Address: 40124 Bologna BO, Italy; Via Clavature

A variety of unique little food vendors can be found in the neighborhood along Via Clavature, east of Piazza Maggiore. There are also other little markets on side streets. For instance, the town's oldest fish market, Pescheria Brunelli, is definitely worth a visit. Go inside Mercato di Mezzo if you're in a hurry and need a fast bite. It's a terrific idea to grab some food or drink as keepsakes from this covered market and enjoy a casual meal.

Look Around Santo Stefano Square

Address: Piazza Santo Stefano, 40125 Bologna BO, Italy.

A remarkable collection of interlocking Romanesque churches may be seen in Piazza Santo Stefano, commonly known as Piazza delle Sette Chiese, or The Square of Seven Churches. Roman temple and column remnants are allegedly the foundation for the oldest, the church of Santi Vitale e Agricola. The church bears the names of two saints who, in the time of Roman Emperor Diocletian, were martyrs in Bologna and are thought to have passed away here. A fascinating courtyard with a tangle of tiny chapels is also present.

View the artwork at Bologna's Pinacoteca Nazionale

Address: Via delle Belle Arti, 56, 40126 Bologna BO, Italy

Contact info: +39 051 420 9442

One of the greatest art galleries in Italy is the Pinacoteca Nazionale di Bologna, or National Art Gallery of Bologna. Located in a historic Jesuit building from the 17th century, the museum has been accessible to the public since 1885. It has a sizable collection of oil paintings that date back to the thirteenth century, along with some significant pieces from the Renaissance, Mannerism, and Baroque eras. View works by Italian painters like Titian, Raphael, and the Carracis, then head to the gallery's temporary exhibits. Consider visiting the

Academy of Fine Arts, housed in the same building, after your visit.

See the Oldest University in the World

The University of Bologna is the oldest university in the world, having been founded in 1088. Visit the Museum of Palazzo Poggi, which has fascinating displays on human anatomy, natural history, military architecture, physics, and old maps, even if you're not a student. Or, you may take a leisurely stroll around the oldest botanic gardens in Italy, the Botanic Garden and Herbarium, which was established in 1568. For a more in-depth look at the history of the university, you may schedule a tour, but taking a leisurely stroll around campus is also a fun way to spend an afternoon.

Savor the Aperitivo.

In Italy, the hour before dinner is known as aperitivo, and it usually begins between 6:30 and 7 o'clock. Via Pescherie Vecchie, which is located right off Piazza Maggiore, is the greatest place in Bologna to have an Aperol Spritz or Negroni. Numerous eateries and pubs surround the Boulevard, providing outdoor dining, wines by the glass or bottle, delectable appetizers, and excellent people watching. Mercato Delle Erbe, a food market during the day, transforms into a bustling nightlife attraction with a variety of eateries and food vendors encircling a central dining hall after dark.

Climb Asinelli Tower

Address: P.za di Porta Ravegnana, 40126 Bologna BO, Italy

After indulging in a hearty meal, you can walk the 498 steps to the summit of the 97.2-meter (319-foot) Asinelli Tower to get your exercise. Erected in the twelfth century by the Asinelli family, it stands as the highest point in Bologna and is the tallest leaning medieval tower in the world. You'll be able to see the surrounding countryside from the summit, as well as all of the city's prominent sites. Close by, the considerably smaller Garisenda Tower stands at 47 meters (154 feet) and exhibits a slight lean similar to its sibling. The two together make up Bologna's "Two Towers." Visitors are not permitted on Garisenda Tower due to its steep inclination. On the official website of Asinelli Tower, tickets for the climb can be purchased in advance.

Discover the City's Secret Canals

Venetian canals may be the most well-known in Italy, but perhaps this is only because Bologna's are obscured by adjoining structures. The window on Via Piella, which offers a view of the Canale delle Moline, gives you a glimpse into some of these waterways. Alternatively, think about reserving a hotel room or vacation home with views of the ocean below.

Go inside the San Petronio Basilica

Address: Piazza Maggiore, 40124 Bologna BO, Italy

Contact info: +39 346 576 8400

With its location off of Piazza Maggiore, the Basilica di San Petronio is the oldest church in the city. Built beginning in 1390 and dedicated to Saint Petronius, the patron saint of Bologna, the basilica was not formally consecrated until 1954. See the city's oldest musical institution, the Music Chapel of San Petronia, within its boundaries. Its 552-year-old organ is still in service today. The astronomer Cassini constructed the world's longest sundial, measuring 67.27 meters, and the basilica is home to the Cappella Bolognini, or Chapel of the Three Kings, which features frescoes by Giovanni da Modena on its walls.

Explore the Longest Portico in the World

Address: Via di San Luca, 16–22, 40135 Bologna BO, Italy

The longest portico in the world is the Portico di San Luca, spanning 3.8 kilometers (2.4 miles) and featuring 666 arches. Built in the 1700s and 1700s, it begins at Porta Saragozza and ascends the Colle della Guardia hill to the Sanctuary of the Madonna of San Luca. Constructed to shield the sanctuary's emblem from precipitation during the yearly Feast of the Ascension, the 666 arches—a number commonly linked to "the beast"—were meant to represent the Madonna's triumph over the devil. Nowadays, you can take a car up to the church, but a typical Bolognese experience is to walk the trek.

Look around Neptune Fountain

One of the most well-known icons of the city, the Neptune Fountain, was designed by Giambologna in the latter half of the sixteenth century and is located in the middle of Piazza del Nettuno. A trident-wielding Neptune sits atop a pile of putti and mermaids, who are arranged quite carefully astride dolphins with water shooting from their breasts in this opulent, and at the time of its unveiling, highly contentious, composition. A wall featuring pictures of World War II partisans who lost their lives is next to a memorial honoring those who perished in the 1980 train station bombing, just next to the fountain.

Top Accommodations In Bologna

The majority of Bologna's lodging options are for business travelers, with very few low-cost establishments. Prices can more than treble (March to early May & Sept–Dec) during the trade-fair peak. During certain times, many hotels prefer to accept block reservations, and it can be challenging to make a single reservation. This is the place to stay.

Centro Storico

There are many hotels in Bologna's old center, ranging in class from five-star luxury to upscale business lodging. That is reflected in their price.

Santo Stefano

Compared to the city center, this neighborhood offers slightly more peace and better pricing. Guesthouses, B&Bs, and a more regional experience are probably what you'll discover.

North of The Bologna Centrale

Budget travelers should aim to travel north of Bologna Centrale, namely north of the train station. There are several guesthouses, affordable hostels, and a few upscale business hotels.

Which Season Is Ideal For Traveling To Bologna?

The shoulder seasons of spring and fall are the ideal times to visit Bologna. Enjoy nice weather, less crowds, and the opportunity to see the city at its best during these seasons. During the springtime, from March to May, the city has typical temperatures between 10°C and 20°C (50°F and 68°F), which are perfect for strolling about the streets. Bologna is also best visited in the fall, from September to November, when the weather is often dry and pleasant, with highs of 12°C to 24°C (54°F to 75°F). Bologna is chock full of fresh food events in the autumn, which coincides with harvest season.

How Many Days Would You Need In Bologna?

The majority of visitors spend two to three days exploring Bologna. You have enough time to stroll through the historic core of the city and take in the food markets, medieval architecture, and rich cultural legacy of the area. There will be enough time for you to see famous sites including the Basilica di San Petronio, Piazza Maggiore, and the Two Towers (Asinelli and Garisenda). Don't pass up the opportunity to sample traditional Bolognese cuisine, such as mortadella and tagliatelle al ragù (Bolognese pasta). You can tour at a slower pace and spend more time in the city's museums, like the Museo Civico Archeologico and the Museo d'Arte Moderna di Bologna, if you have three days to spare. You might also use Bologna as a base for a day excursion to Modena or Parma.

THE COMPLETE CINQUE TERRE TRAVEL GUIDE

Cinque Terre, which means "Five Lands" in English, is a group of five settlements in the Liguria region of northwest Italy. It is a national park with colorful buildings cascading down cliffsides into the Mediterranean Sea and terraced farming fields. Although there are only 4,000 people living in the area, three million tourists visit it annually, many of them being day trippers. But a longer stay is warranted at the settlements and the hiking paths that connect them. To fully experience the region, stay for three nights.

Towns in Cinque Terre

Magnamaggiore

Riomaggiore, the southernmost village and the first you'll come across while traveling from La Spezia, is stunning; one of the most well-known sights in the region is its little harbor, which is tucked between the homes. It's a little livelier than the equally lovely but nearby Manarola, with a number of great eateries crammed into the little town; nevertheless, be warned—the area is extremely mountainous. The Via dell'Amore, or the "Road of Love," begins here and winds around the cliff between Riomaggiore and Manarola. There are plans to reopen it in 2024, despite the fact that it has been closed since a landslide in 2012.

Pro Tip: Santuario di Nostra Signora di Montenero is a church set on a rock with breathtaking views of Cinque Terre. It's accessible after a 45-minute trek above town.

Manarola

That famous image of the Cinque Terre, of the coloured buildings falling into a small harbour like a cascade? In the cove somewhat to the north of Riomaggiore, that's Manarola. People here jump into the water from the rocks that surround the settlement; there is no beach. Like Riomaggiore, Manarola is steep, but it's known for its sunsets, which are best viewed from Nessun Dorma, the pub directly below, or from the little park perched on a cliff under the cemetery. Not only is it the starting point of the hiking trek to Corniglia, but it's also where you can catch the bus to Volastra, high on the cliff above.

Pro Tip: Before you head up, stop at Cappun Magru for one of the finest sandwiches you've ever had.

Corniglia

The only settlement among the Cinque Terre that is perched on a cliff is Corniglia; to get there, take a short bus journey or climb 377 steps from the train station. This keeps it marginally less crowded with tourists than the other communities. Still, it's a charming little village, full of picturesque churches, a square crowded with inhabitants, and lots of vantage spots for taking in the views. The most popular stretch of the Sentiero Azzurro is from Corniglia to Vernazza; it's preferable to begin there to avoid the strenuous climb from Vernazza.

Vernazza

The most well-liked of the communities is Vernazza, which has a tiny sandy beach and is presumably due to its relatively level core. Though Manarola and Riomaggiore are packed in between the cliffs, Vernazza is more expansive, with a promontory winding around its charming harbor that serves as a beach. On the opposite side of the promontory is another beach, a dramatic church, and a ruined castle.

Monterosso al Mare

The closest thing to a typical beach resort in the Cinque Terre is Monterosso al Mare, the largest settlement of the region and more akin to a small town than a village. It's comparatively level, with a charming downtown that opens into a sizable sand beach and is packed with cafes and stores. Situated on opposite sides of a cliff are the old center and the "modern" town.

What Is The Cinque Terre And Where Is It?

Established in 1999, the Cinque Terre National Park is the oldest and smallest national park in Italy. It is only 15 square miles in size, yet it is jam-packed with breathtaking scenery, including steep cliffs, picturesque coves, crystal-clear blue waters, terraced vineyards, and olive groves connected by a system of walkways. In northwest Italy, the Cinque Terre are situated directly south of Genoa. Easy access to the mainline train stations in Genoa, Pisa, Rome, Florence, and Nice is provided by this location.

Additionally, a local train runs between La Spezia and Levanto, making stops at each of the municipalities along the way. Although the Cinque Terre is referred to as the "Five Lands" or Cinque Terre in Italian (pronounced "cheen-kweh teh-rreh"), it is actually a length of shoreline along the Italian Riviera made up of five distinct communities. The settlements are Monterosso, Vernazza, Corniglia, Manarola, and Riomaggiore, and they run from north to south. Though they are all stunning, with pastel buildings cascading down the slopes and glittering views of the sea, each of the five has an own personality.

How To Get To Cinque Terre

The relative inaccessibility of Cinque Terre, where the settlements were previously only reachable by water or trail, is part of its allure. There's a road now, but parking is scarce, which adds to the stress of driving. Take the train instead; the Cinque Terre Express stops at every village with only a little distance between each, traveling three times an hour from La Spezia in the south to Levanto in the north. The cost of a ticket is €5 for each trip or €18.20 for the entire day (during the low season, which runs from January to March, it is €14.80). Piesa and Genoa are the closest international airports. From there, you can catch the railway from Genoa or Pisa to La Spezia or Levanto.

Cinque Terre can also be accessed from the water, which is how they were intended to be seen. Ferries leave from La Spezia, Lerici, Portovenere, and Levanto in the summer and stop at all the villages between March and November. Lastly, Explora 5 Terre is a tourist minibus that runs along the shore. The hamlets situated higher up the cliffs can be reached by the hop-on, hop-off service; however, the road trip takes significantly longer than the rail or boat trip. Starting at €18.50 are tickets.

The Best Seasons To Go

The Cinque Terre are never truly calm; Easter through October is when things get busy. But avoid July and August if you want to avoid the worst of the throng. Summertime is not the greatest time to go walking because it may be very hot and dry, with average highs of 29°C/84°F. Accommodations become booked up well in advance.

With pleasant weather and less crowds than during peak season, May and September make up the shoulder season, which is a great time to explore the Cinque Terre. Springtime is primarily dry with average high temperatures of 17–21°C/63–70°F. The rainiest months are October and November, and there's a chance that strong thunderstorms will cause landslips.

You can also score a deal and have the roads to yourself in December and January if you're willing to take a chance during the off-season. However, you run the chance of boats being suspended and hiking trails being stopped in inclement weather, and certain eateries and lodging facilities closing in the winter.

How To Navigate Around The Cinque Terre

Trekking, trains, buses, boats, and cars are the available modes of transportation between the Cinque Terre; although driving within the region is not advised, we will cover it if you choose to do so. You have three pass choices to pick from if you want to travel across the Cinque Terre by bus, train, or foot:

- **The Cinque Terre trekking Card:** The Cinque Terre Trekking Card allows you to ride the buses and access the trekking trails;

- **The Cinque Terre Treno Card:** The Cinque Terre Treno Card allows you to ride the trains and access the hiking trails;

- **Cinque Terre Express:** These are essentially the single train fairs, called Cinque Terre Express. Perfect for people who don't want to travel far.

The Cinque Terre might theoretically be explored entirely on foot. Unfortunately, there is only a railway link available as the trail between Riomaggiore, Manarola, and Corniglia is closed. This indicates that just two of the four routes are currently accessible to the general public:

- From Monterosso to Vernazza. (Travel time: 1 hour 30 minutes, 3.5 km / 3.1 mi)

- From Vernazza to Corniglia (1 hour 30 minutes, 4.4 km / 2.4 km).

By the way, the scenery is amazing, so even though the hike is exhausting, we highly recommend it! There is an unofficial hike that passes through the mountain without the need for a pass. While we didn't do it ourselves, we did meet some other tourists who had, and they reported that it was really exhausting (many ups) and that the view wasn't all that exciting because the route went through a mountain rather than by the sea.

The Cinque Terre Treno Card

The Cinque Terre Treno Card is a day pass that costs €11.40 for kids between the ages of 4 and 12 and €18.20 for adults. It includes the following:

- Trains to any of the Cinque Terre departing from La Spezia at any time and arriving in Levanto. Trains run from 4 a.m. till midnight.

- Town buses that operate at any time (but only within the town, not between towns). Very seldom will you need to use them. That is, unless you are in Corniglia, where the station is located far below.

The Cinque Terre Trekking Card

The day pass known as the Cinque Terre Trekking Card costs € 4.50 for kids aged 4 to 12 and € 7.50 for adults. It includes access to the following:

- Town buses that operate at any time (but only within the town, not between towns). Very seldom will you need to use them. That is, unless you are in Corniglia, where the station is located far below.

- Although not very good, the National Park's WiFi is still good enough for WhatsApp conversations.

- Using the pay restrooms at train stations (which are kept in a clean and well-maintained state).

- The hike from one fishing village to another.

Cinque Terre's Express Trains

You can purchase a single rail journey if you do not intend to travel up and down among the communities. Each single journey costs €4 (€2 for children). Consequently, you will not be able to go trekking with it and would have to purchase a ticket for every trip. Each station has a machine where you can purchase them. If you do not intend to travel extensively, it is a wonderful idea to combine the trekking card.

CINQUE TERRE BY BOAT

We heartily suggest taking the Cinque Terre boat tour! There are stops at each village en route to the Cinque Terre and Levanto, such as La Spezia and Portovenere. Being above sea level, Corniglia is simply too far away to halt. For the boat tour, we advise purchasing a day pass, which may be used for the entire day or only the afternoon. Though undoubtedly the most elegant choice, it is not the most affordable.

Costs for a daily boat ticket to see the Cinque Terre:

Daily Ticket:

Adult: €30

Children: (6–11 years old): €15

Afternoon Ticket:

Adult: €23

Children: (6–11 years old): €15

Cinque Terre By Car

Consider first whether it is worthwhile to drive to Cinque Terre if you intend to do so throughout your trip. We considered renting a car to go to Cinque Terre, but after doing a lot of research and speaking with others who had already done it, we realized we would end up in a mess.

We most strongly advise against driving to Cinque Terre. Finding a parking space is a problem, to say nothing of the high cost. You also have to constantly trek up and down the hill because it's a long hike from the towns.

Where To Eat

Eating at restaurants is one of the best parts of visiting the Cinque Terre, as it is with any trip to almost anywhere in Italy. Experience the Cinque Terre like never before by eating seafood straight from the Ligurian Sea, picking produce from the terraced hills around the five charming towns, and sipping locally produced wines from the vineyards that encircle the settlements. When you compare those fine ingredients to the atmosphere of a quaint trattoria or an open-air eatery boasting a breathtaking sea view, you'll understand why so many people consider the Cinque Terre to be among their favorite locations in Italy.

Nessun Dorma

Address: Località Punta Bonfiglio, 19017 Manarola SP, Italy

Contact info: +39 340 888 4133

Manarola's favorite seaside restaurant has a notice that reads, "No pasta or pizza." Rather, Nessun Dorma offers platters of appetizers, or antipasti in Italian, along with house wine or light drinks and a vista fit for a millionaire. Walking enthusiasts can stop in for a quick snack and drink or stay and enjoy a dinner consisting of multiple small dishes due to the restaurant's convenient position right above the Manarola beautiful viewpoint. Get there early if you want the finest sunset view, as they don't take bookings.

Ristorante Miky

Address: Via Fegina, 104, 19016 Monterosso al Mare SP, Italy

Contact info: +39 0187 817608

Many Cinque Terre eateries fill their patrons up with hearty portions of seafood, whether it's fried, sautéed, or included in a pasta dish. The emphasis at Ristorante Miky, a longtime favorite located directly on Monterosso's bustling coastal promenade, is on sophisticated, creatively prepared small meals featuring the best of the Cinque Terre's richness. Grab a seat on the shady front patio and enjoy a Monterosso-style view of the passing scenery.

Trattoria dal Billy

Address: Via A. Rollandi, 122, 19017 Manarola SP, Italy

Contact info: +39 0187 920628

Comfortable Trattoria dal Billy is beautifully positioned at the top of Manarola, amid vertigo-inducing vistas from its terraces or window seats, thanks to a series of stairs. Enthusiasts swarm to this modest eatery for its reasonably priced, expertly prepared, and substantial servings of freshly caught fish. Bonus points for the welcoming personnel as well. Make sure to reserve a table in advance for lunch or dinner.

Rio Bistrot

Address: 19017 Riomaggiore, SP, Italy

Contact info: +39 0187 920616

At Rio Bistrot, you can enjoy elegantly prepared seafood meals and appetizers for lunch or supper. The restaurant has a beachy vibe and a rustic decor made of stone and repurposed wood. Indeed, this is the Cinque Terre; it's touristy, but nonetheless. Try to get a seat at a patio table to see the bustling waterfront of Riomaggiore. Try a tasting menu with wine pairings and have a look at the entire menu for a worthwhile indulgence.

Osteria A Cantina De Mananan

Address: Via Fieschi, 117, 19018 Corniglia SP, Italy

Contact info: +39 0187 821166

Tiny Corniglia is often completely ignored by visitors to the Cinque Terre, or worse, they are passed over completely. They're losing out on the charm of the town and the opportunity to dine at the intimate, congested Osteria A Cantina De Mananan. This restaurant serves straightforward, substantial fish and land-based dishes; the pesto is especially good.

L'Ancora della Tortuga

Address: Salita Frati Cappuccini, 4, 19016 Monterosso al mare SP, Italy

Contact info: +39 0187 800065

Setting: L'Ancora della Tortuga is one of the most romantic, set atop a sea cliff and cut into the slope of Monterosso. The dining area, with its nautical decor, and the patio outside both provide views of the sea. The sweets are mouthwatering works of art, and both land- and sea-based specialties are highly praised by patrons.

Fornaio di Monterosso

Address: Via Fegina, 112, 19016 Monterosso al Mare SP, Italy

Contact info: +39 0187 817420

This straightforward bakery and pizzeria can sustain you from dawn to night, conveniently located near the train station in the newer part of Monterosso al Mare. In the morning, warm baked products such as croissants and cappuccinos, or cornetto (the Italian equivalent), are offered. It's panini and sliceable pizza during noon. Come in after 6 p.m. for freshly cooked wood-fired pizzas.

Il Pescato Cucinato

Address: Via Colombo, 199, 19017 Riomaggiore SP, Italy

Contact info: +39 339 262 4815

Head to this straightforward takeaway place on Via Colombo, Riomaggiore's main street, when you're hungry but don't want to sit down for a formal meal. They serve paper cones full of freshly caught fish and seafood. Avoid omitting the anchovies! You may get a delicious, authentically Cinque Terre dinner to-go by adding fries to your order. There are several options here for vegetarians as well.

A Pie' de Ma'

Address: Via dell'Amore, 55, 19017 Riomaggiore SP, Italy

With a great view of the sea and situated directly above Riomaggiore's train station, this welcoming bar is a great place to stop for a quick glass of wine or to spend more time enjoying a sit-down meal in their restaurant or nibbles and wine tasting. While the restaurant offers a small yet filling menu of pastas, fish, and meat, the menu primarily consists of salads and antipasti dishes.

Gelateria Vernazza

Address: Via Roma, 13, 19018 Vernazza SP, Italy

Renowned for having the greatest artisanal gelato in the Cinque Terre, Gelateria Vernazza is the perfect place to grab some wonderful gelato as a tasty mid-afternoon (or mid-morning, we won't tell) snack or dinnertime treat. Try chocolate and wasabi or chocolate and basil if you're feeling adventurous, or just go with the tried-and-true flavors. Whatever you decide, it will taste great.

Where To Stay In Cinque Terre

The five Cinque Terre villages, one of the most visited places in Italy, are best seen in the late afternoon and early morning after the day-trippers have left. Undoubtedly, you ought to spend the night in order to fully appreciate their exquisite beauty. This guide offers recommendations based on your travel style and budget to assist you in choosing a place to stay in Cinque Terre. As soon as possible when planning your vacation, reserve your Cinque Terre lodging because there is a limited quantity and the best locations go fast. Note that the majority of lodging options in the Cinque Terre are limited to basic bed and breakfasts, private flats, and AirBnBs, many of which have a two-night minimum stay requirement. Most hotels are modest, family-owned businesses.

Where in Cinque Terre can I stay?

NOTE: If you prefer upmarket and luxury accomodation, the Grand Hotel Portovenere is nearby. Luxury accommodations are highly limited.

GUIDE FOR ACCOMMODATION PRICES PER ROOM/NIGHT

Luxurious/Upscale – €210+

Boutique/Midrange: €130-250

Budget: €70–120 for B&B

Ultra-budget / Hostel: €30–45

Where to Stay In Cinque Terre

Everybody has a favorite Cinque Terre village, so it really depends on your vacation itinerary and preferences where you stay. Monterosso is the ideal option if you're on a tight schedule, need to be close to a major train station, and enjoy sandy beaches. Of all the communities, this one offers the widest variety of lodging. The smallest village with the fewest visitors is Corniglia, the ideal choice for those seeking peaceful privacy. Take into account how much luggage you have as well as your capacity to navigate stairs and steep streets both with and without the luggage. Of the villages, Monterosso is the flattest, while Corniglia and Riomaggiore have mountainous topography.

MONTEROSSO AL MARE

Because of its expansive sandy beach, Monterosso is the largest village in the Cinque Terre and a well-liked destination for travelers. Compared to the other towns, there is a greater selection of lodging choices, as well as more dining alternatives and nighttime activities. Many Cinque

Terre boat cruises leave from Monterosso, if that's how you want to view the villages from the water. The train station at Monterosso, the last village before Genoa, is a convenient stopping point for your next adventure. This town is the flattest, making it a suitable option if you have a lot of luggage or have trouble moving around.

Where to Lodge In Monterosso Al Mare

Mid-Range/ Budget-Friendly: Hotel La Colonnina

Savor the rooftop terrace's views of the coastline before retiring to your room to unwind with all the modern amenities, like as air conditioning—which is sometimes lacking in this part of the world. Breakfast consists of freshly baked cakes, and the staff will make you feel very welcome. The motel may be easily walked in ten minutes from the station. There are family rooms available.

Luxurious/Upmarket - Eremo della Maddalena

Perched in the hills with a view of Monterosso is this exceptionally unique guesthouse. Set within a converted hermitage, the exquisitely designed apartments are tucked away among olive groves. Among the amenities is a pool with views of the shore. If you would rather not hike up the steep slope to get to the property, a shuttle is available. There are family rooms and free parking.

Budget: Hotel Souvenir

At this quaint hotel, the economy rooms are a great deal. They are simple but cheerfully furnished, and they provide all you need for a quick visit. The hotel's beach and railway station are both easily accessible, and the cost of the accommodation includes a breakfast buffet.

VERNAZZA

Vernazza is a well-liked destination for lodging in the Cinque Terre and is arguably the most picturesque village. Piazza Marconi and the charming natural waterfront are surrounded by colorful structures. There are two little swimming beaches, and it's easy to reach the trekking routes that lead to Monterosso and the neighboring settlements. As the sun sets in the evening, enjoy a seafood feast at the Belfonte restaurant. Having dinner at this eatery, housed inside an 11th-century castle, while the sun sets, is guaranteed to be the highlight of your Italian vacation.

Midrange: Hotel Gianni Franzi

Known for its prime location beneath Vernazza's Doria castle and its charming terraces where visitors may partake in breakfast and wine tasting, Hotel Gianni Franzi is well-liked. Don't anticipate an opulent stay. There may be multiple flights of stairs to get to your accommodation with amazing views. Rooms are basic with minimal amenities.

Luxury: MaDa Charm Apartment

The majority of lodging options in Cinque Terre might be characterized as rustic. An exception, with air conditioning and contemporary furnishings and amenities, is MaDa Charm Apartment. This apartment is a fantastic alternative for families because it has a fold-out couch bed and a small patio with views of the port below.

Budget B&B: Albergo Barbara

This well-known one-star hotel offers inexpensive accommodations that don't have views. However, if views are what you're looking for, Albergo Barbara also has them, with a view of Vernazza Harbor. The hotel has simple rooms and no elevator, but it has friendly staff and is conveniently located near the railway station.

Budget: La Perla delle 5 Terre

La Perla delle 5 Terre offers simpler, more spacious rooms than most other Vernazza hotels. Families can reserve a triple room, and an elevator is available to access the upper levels. There is a welcoming cafe downstairs for breakfast, and the resort is five minutes from the train station.

MANAROLA

Do you want to capture the ideal Cinque Terre sunset? If so, Manarola might be the ideal location for your visit in the Cinque Terre. Many visitors have a special place in their hearts for Manarola, which is the second village north from La Spezia. This town is surrounded by vineyards and is well-known for its breathtaking scenery and crisp, dry white wines.

Manarola is the starting and finishing point for many of the region's well-known hikes, and images here are sure to be amazing. Manarola has a wider variety of lodging options than the other settlements in the center Cinque Terre. Speaking of those sunsets, Head to Nessun Dorma once the crowds have dispersed for the day and savor a hearty antipasto platter paired with a glass of local wine as the sun sets.

BEST HOTELS AND ACCOMMODATIONS IN MANAROLA

Midrange: Hotel Marina Piccola

Hotel Marina Piccola is a compact hotel with modern amenities and a contemporary feel that underwent recent refurbishment. The air-conditioned rooms feature trendy décor and a refrigerator to store food and drinks. There are accommodations with views of the sea. For families, there are larger accommodations available. Perfectly situated for your stay in Cinque Terre, Hotel Marina Piccola is only a five-minute stroll from the station in the center of the town.

Luxury/ Elegance: La Torretta Chic

Character-filled and housed in a historic edifice is La Torretta. Every room has been exquisitely furnished with designer accents and artwork. Rain showers are available in each bathroom and a Nespresso coffee maker is available for your morning coffee on the balcony. Although there is a slight ascent from the railway station to this boutique hotel, you may make your transfer easier by utilizing the hotel's free luggage transfer service.

Budget hotel: Da Baranin

The Da Baranin offers basic but cozy rooms ten minutes' walk from Manarola station. A sumptuous breakfast is included in the accommodation charge, and certain rooms provide views of the sea. If you are on a tight budget, this is a terrific value resort, however it may not be perfect if you have a lot of luggage or mobility issues due to the steep ascent to the hotel.

Luxurious and romantic suites: The First Manarola

The First Manarola's Royal Honeymoon room is ideal for a honeymoon or anniversary, and it boasts the breathtaking views of the coastline you've ever imagined. Every accommodation at this facility has opulent modern décor, and the largest suite boasts a jacuzzi with views of the sea. The sun-filled patio is the ideal spot to look down at the scenic beach.

RIOMAGGIORE

Typical among the area's medieval villages is Riomaggiore. Clinging to the cliffs, its colorful Case Torre tower residences provide breathtaking views of the coastline and Ligurian Sea. Situated at the southernmost point of the Cinque Terre, this village is frequently visited by tourists as their first port of call before moving on to the next town. Riomaggiore is most picturesque at dawn and twilight, when most visitors have left for the day, which is why it is there. To finish the romantic scene, you can swim at the small stony beach and look up at the old castle. The village isn't the greatest option for people who have problems walking up and down hills because it is centered around a single main cobblestone street that is steeply inclined. It's the ideal town to stay in if you're searching for nightlife while visiting the Cinque Terre, as locals and tourists congregate in the cafés and restaurants till late in the evening.

THE BEST PLACES TO STAY IN RIOMAGGIORE

Midrange – La Cometa di Rio

The deluxe accommodation at La Cometa di Rio has a balcony with views that are authentically Cinque Terrean. This guest home, located in the center of Riomaggiore, offers large, contemporary rooms with couches for guests to unwind on after a strenuous day of touring or trekking. There is a minibar and refrigerator in the room. Although there are pubs and restaurants nearby, this home includes soundproofing for when it's time to go to bed.

Luxury: Terra Prime Suite

You might not want to leave Terra Prime Suite because it has all you need for a comfortable stay in Riomaggiore. A king-sized bed, a separate dining area, a sauna, and a hot tub are all included in the large room. Sunloungers with views of the coastline are available for relaxation on the expansive patio outside.

Budget: Scorci Di Mare

The well-known hotel in Riomaggiore, Scorci Di Mare, is housed in a historic edifice. The apartment boasts spacious rooms with views of the sea and new, contemporary fixtures. Every room has a flat-screen TV and air conditioning, and some even have terraces or balconies. The hotel is just 300 meters from the train station and only a few steps from the beach.

CORNIGLIA

Hikers and anyone looking to get away from the throng want to stay in Corniglia, the smallest settlement. There are several hundred steps leading down to the village from the train station, and ferries do not stop here. Therefore, if you have mobility concerns, this is not the finest Cinque Terre village to stay in. In case you're looking for a suitable place to enjoy the breathtaking coastline while living in a community surrounded by vineyards, you may have found it here.

BEST PLACES TO STAY IN CORNIGLIA

Midrange apartments: Sea View Cornelia

Spacious, contemporary apartments that comfortably fit up to four persons. There are kitchenettes and coffee makers in each flats. The larger unit features a sunlounge and sea view outdoor terrace.

Budget: B&B da Beppe

Choose to stay with Beppe and his daughter Francesca if you want to get to know the locals. The B&B offers a number of basic rooms suitable for families, couples, and lone travelers. There is wifi and air conditioning in every room. There is a cooking space in the family studio where you can make meals.

How Long Should You Spend in Cinque Terre?

If you're pressed for time, you may see each of the five villages in the Cinque Terre in one day by taking the rail or boat between them and spending about an hour in each. Alternatively, begin early and proceed straight through from beginning to conclusion. Additionally, day trips including travel are offered from other Italian cities such as Florence or Pisa. However, you would be wasting the nicest time of day and not really doing it properly.

Villages are crowded with day-trippers between 10am and 4pm; being on the train platform in Monterosso at 4pm reminded me of riding the London Tube during rush hour. However, in the evenings, everything settles down and the atmosphere becomes considerably more laid back. A three- or four-night stay would be ideal if you wanted to have enough time to see each village, go on a few half-day walks, and take a boat ride along the coast. Staying for a few days allows you to see the villages at different times of the day, so you may choose your favorite and return for supper or the sundown. If you have more time, you may go on a lot more walks or explore further by visiting the nearby towns of Portovenere, Levanto, or La Spezia.

THE COMPLETE GENOA TRAVEL GUIDE

Your next trip to Italy should include a stop in Genoa, also known as Genova in Italian, for its stunning scenery, high mountains, and mouthwatering cuisine. The top things to do in Genoa are the focus of this guide. Note that the word is pronounced in English as "Genoa," yet the Italian name for the city is "Genova." Regardless of how long you want to stay, Genoa, the capital of the Liguria region in the northwest of the peninsula, has a lot to offer visitors. You've come to the perfect location if you're thinking of visiting this significant city! Read on to discover the top sights and things to do in Genoa—we've included some of the greatest activities and attractions in this chapter!

Where Is Genoa And How To Get There

Located between the Mediterranean and the Apennine Mountains, Genoa is situated on the coast of the Ligurian Sea. Many nearby regions, including as Emilia Romagna, Piedmont, Lombardy, and Tuscany, are easily accessible by train. Savona, a stunning seaside town with amazing beaches, and La Spezia, which is sometimes referred to as the entryway to the Cinque Terre region, are two significant cities that are near to Genoa.

Lastly, Santa Margherita Ligure is a quaint seaside town located roughly 35 miles from Genoa, renowned for its attractive harbor and stunning coastline. That being said, the most common and fastest way to get from Rome to Genoa is via train. High-speed trains like the Frecciarossa or Italo offer quicker travel times than the direct train, which takes about three to four hours from Rome to Geno. The travel time from Rome to Genoa by bus is around 4 hours, although this might vary based on traffic and stops made along the way. In Italy, FlixBus is a well-known bus company that provides direct service between Genoa and Rome. Another option is to drive (from Rome or anyplace else in the nation). For example, you can rent a car in Rome and head north on the A1 motorway to Genoa. It takes roughly 4 to 5 hours to travel the approximate 445 kilometers between Rome and Genoa.

What To Expect In Genoa

Given its northern location, Italian is the primary language spoken by the people who live in Genoa. Italy uses the Euro as its currency and is a member of the EU and the Schengen area. The majority of employees in the tourism and service sectors speak English almost fluently, demonstrating their high level of proficiency. But in this case, knowing a little Italian might be helpful. Tipping is not required, although it would be appreciated if you could add 10% or round up the bill.

Although food, lodging, and attractions are more reasonably priced in Genoa than in other Italian towns like Venice or Rome, the city is not regarded for being "cheap." Though it's a fairly safe city, pay attention to your surroundings when wandering, especially at night. Old Town in Genoa is a labyrinth of dark, winding lanes that are tolerant of prostitutes, and there are occasionally muggings that take place there. As in many Italian cities, be cautious of negligent drivers near pedestrian crossings.

When Is The Best Season To Visit Genoa?

Generally speaking, we could recommend visiting Genoa in the warmer months of the year, though the answer to this question would depend on your interests and the things that most interest you. For example, the city comes alive with tourists in the spring when the weather is normally moderate and the temperatures are nice. The weather is ideal for taking in the city on foot, visiting sights, and engaging in outdoor activities without the throngs of people that come with summer. Summer is excellent from June to August. Although it can get very hot and muggy at times, having the sea close by provides a cooling wind, particularly in the late afternoons.

Summertime is the best time to take in the stunning Ligurian coastline, go boating, and lounge on the beaches. Higher lodging costs and larger crowds are to be expected at this time. Autumn brings lower weather from the end of September through November, but it's still a terrific time to explore the city and enjoy outdoor activities. Harvest festivals and culinary activities are another feature of the fall season.

Genoa experiences warm winters with occasional rain. Even though it's the off-season for travel, Genoa still has a lot to offer in terms of historical monuments and museums. Lastly, the city's ambiance is enhanced by the markets and beautiful decorations that the Christmas season offers.

Why You Should Visit Genoa

Not only is this area close to the more well-known Cinque Terre, but there are also other excellent reasons to explore this underappreciated area. One of the main attractions in the region is Genoa's Historic Center, also referred to as Centro Storico locally. This area is a UNESCO World Heritage Site with amazing medieval architecture. The amazing aquarium in Genoa, which is regarded as one of the biggest and most prominent in all of Europe, is another factor in people's decision to visit.

Wine and food can be great excuses to explore the city. Genoa is renowned for its delectable food, especially its seafood specialties and its pesto sauce, which is made from basil bushes that grow in the Ligurian hills. Check out some of the more classic Genoese dishes for more ideas. In addition, there are lively food markets and Vermentino, the crisp white wine produced in the region, is one of the world's best labels. The city has amazing street art, with vibrant murals and other urban artworks along the streets. Genoa will be a fantastic trip if you love photography or just want to learn more about this popular form of artistic expression.

As if everything that has been said wasn't enough, there are fantastic beaches along the coast, and a short drive away are breathtaking seaside towns like Sanremo, Portofino, Lerici, and the Cinque Terre. Having gained an understanding of the city's appeal, let's explore the most captivating activities available in Genoa, Italy.

Top Activities in Genoa

These are a few of Genoa's top attractions and activities, listed in no particular order:

Explore Port Genoa's Attractions

Known locally as the Port of Genova, this seaport is one of the biggest and busiest in all of Europe. It has a lengthy history that dates back to antiquity and confronts the Ligurian Sea. The port has contributed significantly to the growth of the local economy and maritime traffic. Some of the greatest restaurants in town are located along the pedestrian walkway along the harbor, which also provides quick access to a number of Genoa's sites and attractions.

Acquario di Genoa: The Acquario di Genoa is a large aquarium with a wide variety of marine life, including dolphins, sharks, penguins, and tropical fish. It is situated near the harbor. In addition to informative displays and interactive exhibits, visitors can watch animal feedings.

Galata Maritime Museum (or Sea Museum –Museo del Mare): The Galata Maritime Museum, also known as the Sea Museum – Museo del Mare, is another portside attraction that features interactive exhibits on the city's maritime history along with historical artifacts and ship models.

Biosphere: The Biosphere, located near the harbor, is a distinctive glass and steel sphere that holds a tropical garden that symbolizes many ecosystems from throughout the globe. While exploring the rich greenery, visitors can discover the value of biodiversity.

The Large Panoramic Lift: Regarded as a landmark in the port region, this structure offers the most breathtaking views of Genoa and the surrounding coast. You may take in a 360-degree panoramic view of the city and the Ligurian Sea by riding the elevator to the summit.

Porta Siberia and the Lighthouse: The lighthouse, Lanterna, which dates back to the 16th century and is among the highest lighthouses in the world, is situated next to the historic gate known as Porta Siberia, which serves as the entryway to the port region. In case you were wondering, you can get a bird's-eye perspective of Genoa and the port by scaling the top of the Lanterna.

Porto Antico: Translates roughly into the old port ion English. After a day at the beach, take a stroll around the Old harbor, also known as Porto Antico, a quaint neighborhood within the harbor that has been rebuilt with restaurants, cafes, boutiques, and pedestrian promenades. Enjoy riverside eating and take in the nautical ambience. If you're lucky, you might even come upon a replica of Christopher Columbus's renowned flagship, the "Nao Santa Maria," which he used on his maiden voyage to the Americas in 1492. This model is available for you to explore and learn about Columbus, the most renowned citizen of Genoa, and his voyages across the

Atlantic Ocean. You can occasionally find it in the Port of Genoa as part of exhibitions or maritime events.

Visit the Historic Center.

The historic core, sometimes called Centro Storico or Genoa's Old Town, seamlessly blends with the harbor of Genoa and presents a distinctive variety of maritime architecture. The rich history and cultural legacy of the city are on display in this lively and quaint neighborhood. Listed as a UNESCO

World Heritage Site, it is one of Europe's best-preserved medieval cities.

The district, with its winding lanes, alleyways, and charming squares, is a tribute to the historical significance and diversity of the city's architecture. It is lined with stunning buildings ranging from Renaissance palaces to Baroque churches and neoclassical façade.

There are a lot of squares in the historic center that act as meeting places for the locals. Piazza De Ferrari, the main plaza, is a busy center with a famous fountain that is encircled by striking structures like the Teatro Carlo Felice and the Palace of the Doges. Several palazzi, or aristocratic mansions that belonged to noble families during the city's golden age, may be found in this area of town. These palaces, which include Palazzo Ducale, Palazzo Reale, and Palazzo Spinola, are today home to galleries, museums, and other cultural organizations. Visitors can take in the opulent interiors and impressive art collections of these buildings.

Once known as Strada Nuova, Via Garibaldi is a well-known street in the historic center that is well-known for its magnificent palaces. Magnificent Renaissance and Baroque structures, such Palazzo Rosso, Palazzo Bianco, and Palazzo Doria Tursi, border the avenue. The public can view the vast art collections housed within the Strada Nuova Museums, which are made up of these palaces collectively.

Check out Genoa's Carruggi

Carruggi, as they are known across the Liguria region, are the typical small, twisting lanes that have grown to be recognizable as a key component of the historic center. There are many stores, boutiques, cafés, and restaurants lining these old streets. Finding hidden jewels and becoming fully immersed in the local culture can be enjoyed while exploring the carruggi. You should think about scheduling a tour similar to this one if you wish to search for hidden treasures with a local guide.

Visit the San Lorenzo Cathedral.

Situated in the core of Genoa's old district, the Cathedral honors Saint Lawrence. The cathedral, with its Romanesque style, is arguably one of the most attractive structures in the entire city. Along with significant religious artifacts and artwork, the ecclesiastical structure is home to the Sacra Sindone (Holy Shroud). This magnificent structure dates back to the 12th century, and it has an amazing front with a wide range of decorative embellishments.

The cathedral's main entrance is ornamented with a lavishly decorated portal that features scenes from biblical literature. Multiple arches surround the central gateway, and a spectacular rose window composed of intricately carved stone tracery that forms geometric patterns sits atop it. A large number of statues and sculptures adorn the facade.

The facade's structure, which consists of alternating layers of black and white marble to create a visually arresting pattern and is an incredible example of local artistry and skill, is what makes it stand out the most.

Learn about the Palazzi dei Rolli.

The Palazzi dei Rolli, a collection of Renaissance and Baroque palaces that served as the noble families' homes during Genoa's Republic era—a period in the city's history when it was a potent naval stronghold—are also located in Genoa. A UNESCO World Heritage Site, the Palazzi dei Rolli are notable for their architectural and historical significance.

The lists (or "Rolli") made in the sixteenth century to decide which palaces were appropriate for state visits by notable visitors are referred to by this word. It was mandatory for the palaces mentioned in the Rolli to offer adequate lodging for visiting sovereigns, wealthy merchants, and ambassadors in the Republic.

A variety of architectural styles, such as Renaissance, Baroque, and Mannerist, are all present in them. They provide an intriguing labyrinthine feeling as they are strewn around Genoa's ancient center, populating the narrow streets (carruggi).

With their opulent façade, ornate embellishments, extensive paintings, and exquisite courtyards, all of these buildings were designed to symbolize the wealth and power of Genoa's noble families. There are gardens and balconies in some palaces as well. Genoa commemorates the "Rolli Days" in May each year, when some of the city's palaces are free to visit for the general public. Visitors are welcome to tour these historic houses' interiors and take in their aesthetic and architectural marvels during this event.

Head out to the beach.

Since Genoa is a seaside city, there are many opportunities to visit the beach, where it's simple to locate a place to unwind, swim, and soak up the Mediterranean sun. There are possibilities to meet varied preferences within a short distance from the old historic town, whether you prefer rocky coves or sandy beaches.

Some of the beaches you can visit are as follows:

Boccadasse: This sleepy suburb, which is east of Genoa's downtown, has eateries and cafes along with a quaint pebble beach and colorful buildings surrounding the shore.

Nervi: Nervi is a neighborhood with a long stretch of rocky coastline, little bays, and crystal-clear waters. It is located roughly 9 kilometers east of Genoa's city center. The region is well-known for its lovely gardens, beach promenade, and the well-known Passeggiata Anita Garibaldi, a picturesque cliffside promenade.

Immerse Yourself in Genoa's Rich Cultural Events

Throughout the year, Genoa is home to a number of cultural events, such as festivals, concerts, and exhibitions. An annual event, the Genoa International Boat Show draws boaters from all over the world.

Make Out Some Time to Sample the Regional Foods

When in town, make sure to try some of Genoese food's most famous dishes, such as pesto Genovese and focaccia Genovese, which accentuate the flavors of the sea and the abundant produce of the region. Genoese cuisine often emphasizes fresh and uncomplicated ingredients. As you can see, there are many reasons to travel to Genoa—a stunning Italian city with a fascinating and rich past, stunning architecture, and distinctive culinary customs—all just a short distance from the sea!

Top Accommodations in Genoa

Even if it's not the most visited city in Italy, there are still plenty of excellent lodging options to suit all interests and budgets. Based on location and online evaluations, the following are some of the greatest places to stay in Genoa:

Budget- Ostello Bello Genova: With free WiFi and an on-site fitness center, this hip hostel is conveniently located near the Genova Piazza Principe train station. Look here for availability and costs.

Mid-range- B&B Hotel Genova City Center: This excellently situated B&B is cozy and easily accessible from several of Genoa's top attractions. Air conditioning and Wi-Fi are highlights. Look here for availability and costs.

Luxury- Grand Hotel Savoia: This five-star hotel is the only choice if you want your stay in Genoa to be one to remember. With a pool and spa, among other amenities, this 19th-century building serves as the backdrop. Look here for availability and costs.

How Much Time Will You Need In Genoa?

If all you have time for, you may see the majority of the important attractions in a single day because of the city's compact size, which is attributed to the fact that most of the major sites are concentrated near the harbor and in the ancient old town. Three days is the perfect amount of time to explore Genoa if you have more time.

THE COMPLETE LAKE GARDA TRAVEL GUIDE

Italy's largest lake is called Lake Garda. There is enough to keep you occupied for days here, including vibrantly colored villages, castles and Roman ruins, beaches and vineyards, historical monuments, and amusement parks. Although there is a lot to do at Lake Garda, we only highlight the must-see attractions in our guide.

Where Is Lake Garda Located?

Priorities first! Let's locate Lake Garda precisely on a map of Europe and Italy. Northern Italy is home to Lago di Garda, as it is known in Italian. It forms the natural boundary between the three Italian regions of Trentino-Alto Adige to the north, Veneto to the east and southeast, and Lombardy to the west and southwest. Because of this, the lake is an excellent choice if you're want to visit as much of Italy as you can in a short period of time, including its many regions.

The top portion of Lake Garda is long and thin, and it points north. With reckless abandon, its lower southern half sprawls out. The mountain peaks that around the lake get taller and more rugged the further north you go along its shoreline. Expect steep ranges covered in olive trees and vineyards to the south, then plains that extend in the direction of Brescia and Verona.

Best Time To Visit Lake Garda

The shoulder seasons of spring and autumn are the ideal times to explore Lake Garda. In comparison to the busiest summer months, April through June and September through October offer lovely, temperate weather and less tourists. You may take in the beauty of the lake and its surrounds throughout these seasons without feeling overpowered by big crowds. The gorgeous scenery of blooming flowers and verdant foliage in the springtime makes for an idyllic setting for seeing the quaint lakeside towns. In general, the weather is pleasant for outdoor pursuits including cycling, hiking, and boat cruises.

Autumn is a great season for leisurely walks and picturesque drives around the lake, as the region's colors change to gorgeous shades of crimson and gold. As long as the weather stays nice, you can still enjoy being near the sea and taking in the calm atmosphere.

July and August are the best months to visit if you want a livelier vibe and don't mind bigger crowds. The weather is warm and ideal for swimming and tanning. But bear in mind that during this busy season, lodging may cost more and the famous tourist destinations can get very packed.

Is a Trip To Lake Garda Worth It?

One of the main attractions in Northern Italy is Lake Garda. It is the most beautiful lake in Italy because to its picturesque surroundings, quaint lakeside villages, and an extensive array of attractions. A wonderful location for a day trip, weekend getaway, or extended vacation, Lago di Garda is easily accessible from several major Italian towns, such as Venice and Milan. Experience the Italian dolce vita firsthand, enjoy local specialties and highly valued wines, relax on the beach, and have fun at some of Italy's top theme parks.

Anticipate arrogant castles, nationally significant landmarks, medieval villages, magnificent botanical gardens, thrilling treks, and vantage points providing breathtaking panoramic vistas. The lake is a hive of exciting activities and events during the peak season. Ice rinks, holiday marketplaces, and Nativity scenes are common during the winter. Whatever you are looking for, Lago di Garda has a lot to offer. Going to the lake to take in its atmosphere, history, and natural beauty can end up being your favorite part of your vacation in Italy.

How to Get There

The airport in Verona-Villafranca is only 20 kilometers away from the lake. Regular buses travel from the airport to Verona and Mantua. By train, Peschiera del Garda is just fifteen minutes from Verona.

Hourly trains run in both directions between Desenzano del Garda and Peschiera del Garda, which are connected to the Milan-Venice train route. Additionally, Verona offers great train connections, which facilitate the planning of day trips to the city.

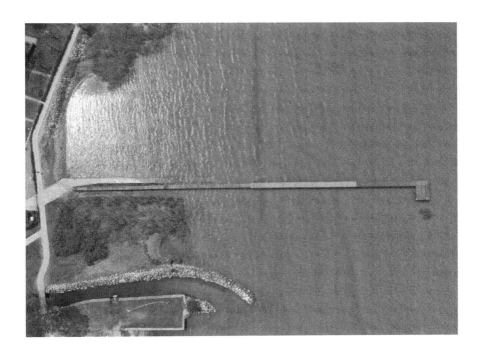

Top Airports To Access Lake Garda

The closest airport to Lake Garda is Verona Airport. Situated just off the lake's southern coast, it offers convenient bus and railway access to the towns along the lake. There are seven other airports that provide fast access to the lake; the one that is most convenient for you will depend on your airline, departure location, and Lago di Garda destination.

Bergamo Orio al Serio, Bologna Guglielmo Marconi, Treviso Antonio Canova, Milan Malpensa, Milan Linate, and Innsbruck Airport are the ones that they are.

How To Get Around

There are several ways to get to Lake Garda, such as convenient bus routes, first-rate boat services, and breathtaking road trips. The route around Lake Garda is as follows.

By Bus:

All three shores have regular bus service on the major thoroughfares.

By boat:

The most leisurely mode of transportation is by boat, with various tour and nighttime cruise services available in summer, as well as at least hourly boat services connecting the main resorts.

By Car:

There are two car ferries that traverse the lake: Limone-Malcesine and Maderno-Torri del Benaco. Wintertime service reductions are substantial; Wnavigazionelaghi.it provides comprehensive real-time information on these services.

The picturesque lakefront route, which only has one lane in each way and frequently winds through tunnels and villages, sees high traffic on summer weekends. All of the villages have pay and display parking, however during the summer months, lines may form.

Top Activities In Lake Garda

Lake Garda is a paradise waiting to be discovered, with its pristine waters mirroring the surrounding landscapes, historic villages tucked away along its beaches, and an abundance of activities for any traveler. This charming location offers the best of both worlds, whether your taste is for outdoor adventures like windsurfing, trekking, and sailing, or you'd rather indulge in regional wines and delicious cuisine in charming piazzas. Get ready to be enthralled by Lake Garda's unique combination of unhurried elegance, cultural diversity, and breathtaking scenery.

Activities in Lake Garda

These are the top activities in Lake Garda, which include experiencing local food, participating in water sports, and touring historic lakefront communities.

1. Head for striking Sirmione

At the base of the lake, Sirmione's long, narrow cape is dotted with hotels that lead to the incredibly charming village that is reached through the ruins of an old castle. Many people visit this popular spa in northern Italy to take a dip or spend the day in the health and beauty center.

It's in a striking site, yet the ice cream parlors and the strain of a million overnight guests each year make the narrow cobblestone passageways creak. It's better to continue walking through the village's congested alleyways, past the ferry terminal on Piazza Carducci, and towards the grassy park and hills covered in cypress trees at the tip of the peninsula.

2. Wander around the angular towers of Rocca Scaligera: Sirmione's idyllic appearance is largely due to the castle that resembles a fairy tale at its entrance. Constructed during the 13th century as the Della Scala/Scaligeri family of Verona grew and strengthened their domain, the boxy towered Rocca Scaligera is nearly encircled by water.

The thirteenth century is when it was created. You are allowed to walk about the walls (the enclosed harbor is particularly picturesque) and climb the towers; 77 steps take you to the keep, and another 92 lead to the top of the highest tower, which offers breathtaking views over Sirmione's roofs.

3. Visit Grotte di Catullo's ruins, a Roman villa from the first century BC/AD.

The Grotte di Catullo, the remnants of a first-century BC/AD Roman villa supposedly belonging to Roman poet Catullus (though there is no evidence to support this claim), is located at the far end of the promontory, a delightful fifteen minutes' walk from the castle. The remains are beautiful, with amazing views across the lake, and are strewn among old olive trees. There is an archeological museum on the site that holds artifacts and pieces of frescoes that have been found nearby.

4. See the most scenic villages

Take a voyage of discovery and discover the fascinating communities that line Lake Garda's coastline. Every village offers a taste of the rich history and culture of the area along with its own distinct charm. Among the most delightful villages to explore are:

Sirmione: Visit the mediaeval castle, unwind in the thermal springs, and stroll through the bustling cobblestone streets of Sirmione.

Malcesine: Take the cable car up Monte Baldo for sweeping views, then stroll around the charming alleyways lined with vibrantly colored buildings in Malcesine.

Riva del Garda: Explore the beautiful Varone Waterfall, the seaside promenade, and the historic fortress of Riva del Garda.

Bardolino: Visit the regional vineyards to sample the well-known wine, take a leisurely stroll along the promenade by the lake, and discover the quaint town center.

Lazise: Relax at cafes by the lake, take in the 14th-century church, and see the old walls.

Limone sul Garda: Discover the charm of Limone sul Garda, a town known for its lemon gardens, winding lanes, and vividly colored homes that cascade down the mountainside.

Every village has its own unique appeal that lets you take in the stunning scenery, try some of the regional cuisine, and feel the warmth of Lake Garda hospitality in some of its most endearing settings.

5. Take a Dip at Lido delle Bionde

A walkway leads to the Lido delle Bionde, a shingle beach where you can eat, drink, swim in the lake, and sunbathe on the adjacent rocks, part of the way down to the Roman remains. Alternatively, head to the village's public beach by turning right when you get to the water, where there's space for paddling as well.

6. Take a ride around the lake by car.

A road drive encircling the lake offers an enthralling fusion of scenic panoramas, quaint towns, and unspoiled natural splendor. You will be rewarded to constantly shifting views of the scene's imposing mountains, undulating hills, and glistening clear waters as you meander along the lake's edge. Discover quaint lakeside towns like Sirmione, which has a mediaeval castle and hot springs, or meander through Limone sul Garda's winding alleyways, where the brightly colored homes appear to tumble down the slope.

Visit secret coves, historical monuments, and neighborhood trattorias to sample real Italian food. The road journey provides an immersive immersion into the essence of Lake Garda's alluring landscapes and quaint culture, in addition to being a picturesque drive.

7. Visit the theme parks Canevaworld and Gardaland

All ages can enjoy a fun-filled day at the theme parks located around the southeast corner of the lake. The largest theme park in the region is called Gardaland, and it is adjacent to the little but well-designed SeaLife aquarium. It's expensive but well-designed, with lots of shade, water activities, and rides suitable for kids as young as three. Take the complimentary shuttle bus that departs from the 2 km away Peschiera train station, or pay extra for parking.

BEST HIKES AROUND LAKE GARDA

Hikers will find Lake Garda to be a haven, surrounded by gently sloping hills and rugged mountain peaks. Its verdant coastlines are home to hundreds of pathways that let you see some of Italy's most breathtaking panoramic vistas and get up close and personal with nature.

The greatest places to go trekking and the hiking routes that surround Italy's largest lake are listed below:

Monte Baldo: A high, lofty mountain called Monte Baldo shoulders Lake Garda's eastern shore. It is crossed by numerous trails with varying degrees of difficulty. Hike here to the Tibetan Bridge for a simple workout. The climb to Naole's Crest is also a favorite of mine because of the springtime wildflower blooms and the sweeping vistas it provides across the lake.

Rocca di Garda: The village of Garda is positioned behind the towering hill known as Rocca di Garda. The nicest views of the lower portion of the lake can be had by hiking to the summit.

Busate-Tempesta Panoramic Path: The Busate-Tempesta Panoramic Path is a dizzying climb that rises above the lake's azure waters. A portion of the path goes up and down a series of metal steps that are fastened to the steep rocks.

Strada del Ponale: Without a doubt, the most breathtaking climb in Upper Garda is the Strada del Ponale. Lake Ledro is a small but exquisitely beautiful lake that may be visited in the Ledro Valley, which is connected to the town of Riva del Garda by this old panorama road.

Where To Stay In Lake Garda

In the summer, practically all of Lake Garda's towns have occupancy rates close to 90%, thus reservations in advance are crucial. Great options abound, but there aren't many affordable lodgings, ranging from fancy hotels to farmstays and campgrounds. Shoulder seasons are when deals are found. These are the top accommodations in Lake Garda.

Aristotle

Sirmione: A charming peninsula that juts into the lake and is well-known for its ancient castle and thermal springs, provides a charming and enchanted environment along with some exquisite luxury hotels.

Malcesine: Malcesine, at the base of the Monte Baldo mountains, offers a variety of family-run hotels and B&Bs, as well as cobblestone streets, medieval buildings, and a magnificent castle.

Riva del Garda:

This hamlet, which sits at the lake's northernmost point, has affordable backpacker lodging, a youth hostel, and contemporary hotels.

Garda:

Garda, which takes its name from the lake, has family-run guesthouses and boutique hotels. Its picturesque promenade is lined with a row of apartments and vacation homes.

Desenzano del Garda:

The major town on the southern bank of the lake features various spas and elegant hotels with views of the lake.

Limone sul Garda:

This quaint village, which is famous for its lemon gardens, is tucked away between a lake and steep cliffs. It features affordable lodging options, family-run inns, and a campground.

How Many Days Should I Spend In Lake Garda

In one to two days, one can have a quick peek at Lake Garda's splendor. Focus on taking a boat excursion, enjoying the lakeside ambiance, and visiting one or two charming towns, like Sirmione and Desenzano del Garda, during your brief vacation. Adding an extra day or two to your visit will allow you to fully experience Lake Garda and its environs. Along with exploring the various cities and villages that dot the lake's shoreline, you may also engage in water sports like paddleboarding or windsurfing.

There's also enough time to take the Funivie di Malcesine cable car up to Mount Baldo. Spending five to seven days in and around Lake Garda will provide you an immersive experience that includes all of the aforementioned activities as well as some downtime by the shore.

THE COMPLETE TRAVEL GUIDE FOR VISITING THE DOLOMITES

The Siltstones. Hiking paths link tiny hamlets and villages, cable cars transport hikers and skiers to the highest mountain summits, and mountain lodges and cottages are scattered throughout verdant, undulating slopes. One of Europe's most breathtaking tourist destinations is the Dolomites, which are found in northeastern Italy. For many travelers, including us, this area of Italy is the high point of the vacation. A magical place is created by the stunning scenery, quaint towns, and an extensive network of amazing hiking routes.

To a first-time visitor, the Dolomites may appear complicated on a map. It can seem overwhelming to know how to plan a trip to the Dolomites because of its topography, winding roads, extensive to-do list, and variety of lodging alternatives. We strive to dispel this uncertainty and address some questions you may not have known you had in this tutorial.

So, What And Where Are The Dolomites?

In northeastern Italy, there is a mountain range called the Dolomites. This mountain range crosses three Italian regions (Veneto, Trentino-Alto Adige/Südtirol, and Friuli Venezia Giulia) and seven Italian provinces (South Tyrol, Trentino, Verona, Vicenza, Belluno, Udine, and Pordenone). This vast mountain range, which was recognized as a UNESCO World Heritage Site in 2009, is among the top destinations for trekking and skiing worldwide.

Our favorite place in the world to hike during the summer is the Dolomites. An extensive array of breathtakingly beautiful and unforgettable paths are available within a very compact area. Later on in this tutorial, we'll discuss these. The Dolomites are a top-notch skiing destination in the winter. So excellent, in fact, that Cortina d'Ampezzo will hold the

Winter Olympics in 2026. The carbonate rock known as dolomite, which makes up the rocky peaks in this region, is the source of the term "Dolomites."

A Brief Geographical Overview on The Dolomites

Numerous mountain groups that rise up from the valleys make up the Dolomites, including the Sella Group, the Odle/Geisler Group, and the Croda da Lago group. Small towns and the highways connecting them can be found within the valleys. The Dolomites are occasionally divided into the eastern Dolomites and the western Dolomites to make geography easier to understand. The border between these two regions is Val Badia.

In the eastern area of the Dolomites, you will find:

- Cortina d'Ampezzo
- Tre Cime di Lavaredo
- Lago di Braies
- Lago di Misurina
- Passo Giau
- The Cinque Torri
- Lagazuoi
- Croda da Lago and Lago Federa
- Selva di Cadore

And to the west, you'll find:

- Val Gardena

- The Puez-Odle Nature Park
- Alpe di Siusi
- Val di Funes
- Sassolungo
- Marmolada
- Seceda
- Sciliar-Catinaccio Nature Park

Getting To The Dolomites

Since there isn't a single official transportation hub or recognized "Dolomites Airport," there are really multiple ways to get to the area. The following is a list of the best cities and airports for flights, along with the estimated travel times to the two locations that serve as the primary "gateways" to the Dolomites (and where you should probably spend the first night):

- **Verona (Valerio Catullo Airport):** Two hour drive to Bolzano, a three hour drive to Cortina d'Ampezzo.

- **Innsbruck (in Austria):** Ninety minutes to Bolzano, Three hours to Cortina d'Ampezzo.

- **Venice (Marco Polo or Treviso Airports):** Three hours to Bolzano, Two hours to Cortina d'Ampezzo.

- **Milan (Malpensa or Bergamo Airport):** Three+ hours to Bolzano, Five hours to Cortina d'Ampezzo.

- **Trieste:** Three hours to Bolzano, three hours to Cortina d'Ampezzo.

- **Bologna:** Three+ hour drive to both Bolzano and Cortina d'Ampezzo.

- **Munich:** Munich ight e just three hours by car but the caveat is that you have to purchase an Austrian highway "vignette" for €9 at a gas station right before you cross the border. Munich is three hours distant by automobile.

The Dolomites are ideal for a road trip (more on that later), and the most convenient way to continue into the heart of the area is to rent a car when you arrive at the airport. Train travel is an option as well, but be advised that it typically requires one or more connections and takes three to five hours.

Consequently, we advise you to quickly check the availability and pricing of car rentals in the Dolomites for your desired dates before deciding on your travel plan. You may discover that hiring a car in Innsbruck, Austria to cross into Italy may cause problems for some rental companies (or increase expenses), and that the alternatives and costs vary sufficiently between two airports to make the overall cost considerably different. There may also be airports that are slightly more conveniently located for access, depending on which area of the Dolomites you're seeking to get to first, or base yourself in.

- We always search and reserve our Italian car rentals with AutoEurope. But because costs have been rising recently, it's a good idea to also look at Rentalcars.com.

- Check out the timetables and purchase tickets for trains on Trenitalia or Omio. Flixbus is the most affordable bus travel alternative.

Main Towns In The Dolomites Region

The Dolomites are home to numerous tiny settlements. We've highlighted a handful of the bigger ones below that are excellent starting points for region exploration.

CORTINA D'AMPEZZO

One of the greatest locations to stay in the Dolomites is this one. There are several hotels and restaurants in this sizable town, some of which have been awarded Michelin stars. Thanks to its ideal location close to Tre Cime di Lavaredo, Lago di Sorapis, the Croda da Lago Circuit, and Lagazuoi, this town is a perfect base from which to explore the Dolomites. Stroll down Corso Italia, the pedestrian thoroughfare that circles the city center of Cortina d'Ampezzo. Take a shopping trip, see the Basilica Minore dei Santi Filippo e Giacomo, and take the cable car to Tofana di Mezzo or Faloria.

SELVA DI CADORE

It was during our first trip to the Dolomites that we stayed in this tiny village. Selva di Cadore is a decent option to consider if you could only choose one place to stay because of its rather central location.

DOBBIACO

Dobbiaco is situated in the Dolomites' northern region. While it's a fantastic starting point for exploring the Lago di Braies and trekking Tre Cime di Lavaredo, getting to most other parts of the Dolomites will require a lengthy trip.

SELVA DI VAL GARDENA & ORTISEI

The Puez-Odle Nature Park is not far from these two settlements, which are situated in Val Gardena. Similar to Cortina d'Ampezzo, there are plenty of lodging options and dining establishments. You may trek the Puez-Odle Altopiano and visit Seceda, Val di Funes, and Alpe di Siuis from this location.

BOLZANO

Located on the western border of the Dolomites is the little city of Bolzano. Although it will take a long journey to go everything, I wouldn't advise staying here. However, this location serves as a gateway to the Dolomites thanks to the train station. You can rent a car from Bolzano for a few days and take a road trip across the Dolomites.

How To Get Around The Dolomites

One of the greatest locations for a road trip if you enjoy them is the Dolomites. One of the finest ways to view the region's astounding selection of sights is by vehicle. We've now taken several road trips through the Dolomites, each to a different region, and it's truly a captivating place to drive through;

every turn in the road offers a new, breathtaking view, every mountain pass is more captivating than the last, and every valley has more charming towns to explore. Owning a car gives you the freedom and flexibility to fully explore the area and see the most famous Dolomites attractions in a reasonably priced and effective manner.

It's also one of the best places we've drove, despite some driving in this region of Italy being subpar (mainly speeding, so be careful). The roads here are also excellent. There is no predetermined road trip itinerary because of the region's vastness and evident obstacles (hey, really tall mountains!).

Since Bolzano is the starting point for your activities in the Dolomites, we advise renting a car there. As an alternative, you can rent a car in any of the nearby towns and areas, such as Munich, Venice, Verona, and Innsbruck. When making rental reservations, we typically utilize RentalCars.com; you can check rates and availability for Italy here. Depending on the type of automobile, you should budget between £80 and £200 for a seven-day car rental, not including insurance. Remember to carry auto insurance as well (find reasonably priced yearly coverage here).

TIP: Be cautious when driving in the area; speed cameras are essentially all over the place in Val Gardena, Alta Badia, and other Dolomite regions. They are bright orange robots, but you will frequently receive a warning before one approaches. Alternatively, never, ever speed.

BUT PUBLIC TRANSPORT IS ALSO AMAZING

The South Tyrol public transportation system is excellent if you don't want to rent a car or can easily reach the Dolomites via the vast European train network. Anywhere you want to travel, whether it's Val di Funes, Lago di Braies, or even deep within the Funes National Park, you can easily get it thanks to the region's excellent bus, regional train, and cable car networks. Obtain a South Tyrol Mobilcard for a duration of one, three, or seven days to have access to all other available transportation alternatives around the area. Tickets are available at hotels, ticket machines, and tourist information centers. The südtirolmobil app can be used to get timetables. and range in price for 1, 3, and 7 days from €15, €23, or €28, respectively.

Best Time To Visit

The Dolomites are one of those destinations that you can go to year-round and still have an amazing time. In the summer, it gets very busy. Think packed hotels, crammed parking lots, and snarling traffic. For those who prefer a more sedate atmosphere, September and early October are the ideal months to explore the Dolomites.

The Dolomites are far less busy and have pleasant weather during the shoulder seasons (imagine clear, crisp days and cool mornings). You won't have the trails or attractions all to yourself, but you will still be able to fully appreciate the breathtaking surroundings without having to deal with the crazy summer crowd. If you can't travel in late summer, spring (mid-June to mid-July) is a great time to go since the meadows are covered in vibrant bursts of color from wildflowers, and the highest mountains are still covered in snow, making for the most magnificent backdrops for your adventures.

Not to mention that many of the towns and facilities (hotels, restaurants) close in the off-season, which runs from mid-October to mid-December and from April to June, make the Dolomites a seasonal trip. This doesn't mean you can't travel to the Dolomites during this time; it just means that there might not be as many lodging options available and that chairlifts, gondolas, and other forms of transportation won't be running.

Best Places To Hike In The Dolomites

Tofana

This mountain, which is a well-liked location for trekking in the summer and skiing in the winter, may be reached at its summit by cable car. The Masi Wine Bar and Ristorante Col Druscié 1778, which serves apple strudel and spiked eggnog alongside salads and heartier meals, is located at the first cable car stop.

Lago di Misurina

It takes around 20 minutes by driving from Cortina d'Ampezzo to reach the picturesque Lago di Misurina, where you can view the yellow rehabilitation clinic for kids, which was established since it was thought that the clean mountain air would heal respiratory conditions. At 5,761 feet above sea level, the lake's 1.6-mile edge, which includes picnic areas, is popular with visitors throughout the year. It is also the starting point for trekking the well-known Tre Cime di Lavaredo trail, which starts at the Rifugio Auronzo.

Bragiser Wildsee (Lago di Braies)

The stunning Seekofel massif rises surrounding this Instagram-famous lake, which is particularly captivating in the summer when the sun shines off its green waters. Rent a wooden rowboat (€25 for an hour, €15 every 30 minutes thereafter) and explore the lake; but, due to its popularity, the boathouse frequently runs out of boats by 11 a.m. It's preferable to get there when the boathouse opens at 9:30 a.m. if you don't want to wait. You can also stroll around the edge of the lake, pausing to see the 1904 chapel.

From the south end of the lake, you can access the trails that climb into the mountains for a more challenging hike.

Activities and Attractions in the Dolomites

We've listed some of our top Dolomite travel spots and activities below. for an all-inclusive itinerary of activities in the Dolomites.

Take a Rifugio Stay

Spending the night in a mountain refuge (Hütte, Rifugio) is one of the nicest parts of hiking in the Dolomites. Encountering the blissful landscape while dozing off in a mountain cabin is an amazing experience unto itself. We adore the ambience of the Dolomites' Rifugi. They study route maps, play cards, read, and sip Schnaps. Additionally, you get to meet new people and exchange stories during dinner because you're seated with other hikers.

Observing how the mountains' hues alter during the day is an additional perk of booking a hut. The mountains had a purple hue when we arrived at Rifugio Alpe di Tires/Tierser Alpl in the late afternoon. When the sun rose, they appeared yellow.

Climb up a Via Ferrata

A mountain route known as a "iron way" or via ferrata is guarded by a system of cables, ladders, pegs, and rungs. Through the use of a via ferrata lanyard and climbing harness, hikers can safely navigate through exposed and vertical passageways by gripping and clipping into wires.

Via ferrata climbing originated from necessity during World War I, while being an exciting sport today. In the Dolomites, troops from Italy and Austria-Hungary engaged in combat. To facilitate soldiers' safe and efficient movement at high altitudes, permanent lines and ladders were fastened to the faces of the rocks. Via ferrata routes are rated using two different systems: the Schall grading scale, which grades from

A to F (easy to extremely difficult), and the Smith/Fletcher dual rating system, which grades from 1 to 6 (easy to hard).

The Gran Cir peak in Puez-Odle Nature Park, which is reachable via Passo Gardena, and the Santner Via Ferrata to the Vajolet Towers, which we walked on stage 1 of our 3-Day Rosengarten Dolomites Trek, are excellent options for novice via ferrata climbers. The Sasso Piatto top can be reached via the fantastic Oskar Schuster via ferrata, which is rated as an intermediate (Grade B/C). The Italian Dolomites are home to more than 200 via ferrata paths.

Sentiero Attrezzato are available in addition to via ferrata options. While these "equipped paths" are equipped with steel cables and other tools for security, they are typically less strenuous than via ferrata routes and don't always require a whole via ferrata gear. One excellent example of a Sentiero Attrezzato is the Sentiero Bonacossa, which stretches across the Cadini di Misurina range. On the ascending path leading to Piz Duleda in Puez-Odle Nature Park, there is also a Sentiero Attrezzato.

Walk the Loop Trail around the Lavaredo's Tre Cime.

Hike of the day surpasses all others. The vistas are breathtaking. You might even believe that, given how little effort you put into the trail, you don't deserve them. You deserve them, after all. We also wish you depart. In summary, the climb encircles the famous Three Peaks in the Sesto/Sexten Dolomites (known as Drei Zinnen in German and Tre Cime di Lavaredo in Italian). Approximately 4 hours are needed to complete the 9.7 km circle.

The mountain hut known as Rifugio Locatelli/Dreizinnenhütte, which faces Tre Cime di Lavaredo's northern flank, offers the most breathtaking perspective of the summits. It is also a fantastic location for lunch. You must drive or take the bus to Rifugio Auronzo in Belluno through the Auronzo - Tre Cime di Lavaredo toll road in order to begin this trip.

Insider Tip: After finishing the circle, hike for half an hour to reach the well-known Cadini di Misurina viewpoint.

Learn what wellness truly means in Alta Badia

One of the top places in the Dolomites is Alta Badia, which is tucked away between the Puez Mountains, the Cir summits, the Fanes Group, the Sella Group, and Mount Sassongher. This delightful area in South Tyrol entices with its picturesque landscape, an abundance of hiking paths, and first-rate lodging.

In the Dolomites, Alta Badia is the undisputed queen of wellness and spa hotels. These hotels treat their visitors to a range of indulgences, including delicious half-board menus, substantial wellness and sauna facilities, alpine-chic design, and picturesque sites.

Walk around Val Gardena and Gaze at the beauty of the Seceda Ridgeline

In South Tyrol, the settlements of Ortisei/St. Ulrich, Santa Cristina/St. Christina, and Selva di Val Gardena/Wolkenstein are all part of the Val Gardena/Grödnertal valley. You may use an aerial cableway from these places to reach several plateaus and summits in the Val Gardena Dolomites. The Seceda top in Puez-Odle Nature Park is one of the most exhilarating focal points in the area. The sharp Odle/Geisler peaks, seen from the Seceda ridgeline, like a Swiss Army Knife that is constantly piercing the sky.

The Seceda summit can be reached in a variety of ways. The Ortisei-Furnes-Seceda cableways offer the quickest ascent path to Seceda. The Seceda summit overlook is just a ten-minute stroll from the mountain station. We strongly advise taking the ridge trail to the Forcella Pana/Panascharte gap, then going on to the mountain meadow of Pieralongia and, finally, to the Rifugio Firenze/Regensburgerhütte.

See Lago di Braies, also known as the pearl of the Dolomites.

Lago di Braies, also known as Pragser Wildsee in German, is an alpine lake located in South Tyrol's Braies Valley, which is a tributary of the Upper Puster Valley (Alta Pusteria, Hochpustertal). The breathtaking, picture-perfect backdrop of Lago di Braies is created by the towering massif of Croda del Becco, also known as Seekofel in German and Sass dla Porta in Ladin. Braies Lake is located at the base of this magnificent mountain. It is known as the Peal of the Dolomites for a reason. In addition, Lago di Braies is not a secret, unlike any proclaimed "pearl."

When you visit Lake Braies, you won't be by yourself. Both at 5 a.m. and 5 p.m. Everyone is eager to see this famous location. The lake can be hiked to Hochalpensee (2254 m), Hochalpenkopf (2542 m), Croda delle Becco/Seekofel (2810 m), and Herrnstein (2447 m), but not many visitors are aware of this.

Regulations pertaining to lake access during the peak season (July 10 – September 10) have changed in recent years. Local officials are limiting the amount of personal car traffic in order to safeguard the lake's delicate ecology. You have to reserve and pay in advance for both parking and transportation to the lake if you plan to visit between July 10 and September 10.

Insider Tip: For a breathtaking perspective of Tre Cime di Lavaredo, hike from the Prato Piazza platform to the summit of Monte Specie, or Strudelkopf in German. This is done after seeing Lago di Braies. Hiking the thrilling Gaisl High Trail from Prato Piazza to Ponticello is also another option.

Hike at the Odle/Geisler Peaks' Foot

One of the most visually remarkable mountain groupings in the Dolomites is the sawtooth Odle/Geisler Group. There's no shortage of ways to make these iconic mountains your own. Hiking along the Adolf Munkel Trail along the foot of the Odle Peaks is possible from Val di Funes. In addition to connecting some of the most picturesque alpine pasture huts in the area, such as Malga Casnago/Gschnagenhardt Alm and Geisler Alm, this trail offers breathtaking views of these pinnacles.

The image of Santa Maddalena in Val di Funes, surrounded by the Odle spires, is arguably the most well-known photo motif. To reach the viewpoint, take the Santa Maddalena

Panorama Trail. Hiking to the summit of Tullen in the Odle d'Eores/Aferer Geisler Group is an additional alternative. This remains a trade secret. For those seeking an even more breathtaking view of the Odle Peaks, experienced hikers might opt to attempt the Col dala Pieres summit walk, which begins in Val Gardena.

Explore the Tunnels and Trails of the First World War

The Dolomites formed the front between Italy and Austria-Hungary during World War I. Between 1915 and 1917, the opposing factions fought a bloody mountain war. In order to fortify the border and defend themselves, both forces constructed trenches, tunnels, and trails. These World War I soldiers' efforts are what made the network of trails that exists today so excellent.

The harsh weather presented both troops with the biggest threat during the fight. Avalanches in December 1916 buried 10,000 Italian and Austrian soldiers in two days. Even though it's hard to conceive how a war could be waged in such harsh terrain, this area has a shameful history, as evidenced by numerous sources. To witness wartime trenches, tunnels, trails, and other ruins, hike to:

- The open-air museum at Cinque Torri
- The Tunnels of Lagazuoi
- Monte Piana
- The Circuit Trail at Tofana di Rozes

Tour the Pale di San Martino Alpine Range

It is sometimes forgotten that the Dolomites contain the greatest and possibly most picturesque mountain range. Between Primiero, Vallde del Biois, and Agordino in Trentino and Belluno is Pale di San Martino, or simply the Pala Group. We advise staying at the San Martino di Castrozza resort in Trentino. You can ascend to the Altopiano delle Pale di San Martino, circumnavigate Pala di San Martino, or reach the summit of Cima della Vezzana from this location. To witness the most breathtaking sunset and alpenglow show, go up to Baita Segantini from Passo Rollo. Go to Val Venegia for an exhilarating hike or a leisurely stroll to Rifugio Mulaz.

Take a Hike to Lake Sorapis (Lago di Sorapis)

A glacial lake in the Ampezzo Dolomites' Sorapiss Group is called Lago di Sorapis. Lago di Sorapis, surrounded by rock and woodland and situated in a natural amphitheater, captivates with its rough mountain backdrop and milky-blue color. You may believe that you are staring at a magic potion-filled pool belonging to an enchantress.

The only way to get to Lake Sorapis is on foot. It just takes two hours to go to Lake Misurina from the Passo Tre Croci mountain pass, which is located roughly midway between Cortina d'Ampezzo and the lake. In the direction of Rifugio Vandelli, take path 215 south. Hikers with experience should think about taking the Forcella Marcuoira saddle as a shortcut back to Passo Tre Croci.

The trail around Lake Sorapis is quite well-traveled and packed. If you are looking for walks that are less crowded around Cortina d'Ampezzo, you might want to try these:

- Trail Croda da Lago Circuit
- Tofana di Rozes Circui Trail
- Giau Passo to Mondeval

Experience a Culinary Hike on Alpe di Siusi

At 56 square kilometers, Alpe di Siusi—also known as Seiser Alm in German and Mont Sëuc in Ladin—is Europe's largest high-alpine pasture. Situated far above Val Gardena, Castelrotto, and Siusi, this high-altitude plateau is part of

South Tyrol. This is a terrific place to enjoy delicious meals and drink with easy strolling. From Compaccio/Compatsch, you can take a detour to the gourmet Gostner Schwaige and Rauchhütte alpine pasture huts by following the Hans and Paula Steger Trail towards Saltria.

Aspiring hikers can begin in Compaccio and attempt the circuit hike from Rifugio Bolzano to Rifugio Alpe di Tires. One of the best spots to enjoy South Tyrolean food is at the Tierser Alpl refuge.

Go on a drive through the mountain passes of the Dolomites

You will drive over several mountain passes as you go between the Dolomites' various valleys. These mountain passes are travel destinations unto themselves. There are restaurants, shops, chalets, parking lots, and cableway valley stations located on several passes. It's also important to know that mountain passes serve as trailheads.

- You can hike the circuit trail around Sass de Putia from Passo delle Erbe.

- You can hike to Gran Cir, Sass da Ciampac and Cima Pisciadu from Passo delle Erbe

- Hiking paths lead from Passo Giau to Lago delle Baste, Lago Federa, and the Mondeval plateau.

- You can hike the Kaiserjäger protected path to Lagazuoi from Passo Valparola.

- You can start the Via Ferrata Oskar Schuster and the circle route around Sassolungo from Passo Sella.

- We suggest climbing the Viel del Pan and Alta Via Della Cresta circuit trail from Passo Pordoi.

Where To Stay In The Dolomites

The distances between the main Dolomites attractions may not seem very great on a map, but when you factor in a few tight passes, twisting single-lane roads, and plenty of "I need to pull over and take a picture" moments, you may quickly add an hour or two to your trip.

Choose one or two base towns near the things you want to visit and reserve many nights there to make the most of your stay, so you don't have to spend as much time driving between your chosen locations as experiencing them. We promise you'll be happy you made the choice when, after a long day of hiking, viewing the dawn and sunset, you only need to travel 20 minutes back to your lodging rather than 1.5 hours! Which dolomite bases are the best?

Val Gardena (Ortisei): Adjacent to Val di Funes, Seceda, and Alpe di Siusi

Alta Badia (Colfosco): Near a wide variety of hikes in the Parco Naturale Puez Odle, such as Gran Cir and Piz Boe, is Alta Badia (Colfosco).

Dobbiaco (Toblach) or Cortina d'Ampezzo: Close to Lago di Braies, Lago di Dobbiaco, Lago di Sorapis, Tre Cime di Lavaredo, and Passo Giau.

Among the hotels in the area, we recommend the following:

BUDGET

GRANDPARENTS' HOUSE, ORTISEI: A lovely bed and breakfast in Val Gardena, Grandparents' House, Ortisei has a large bedroom and living area that are ideal for unwinding after a strenuous day of exploring the outdoors.

GARNI EDERA: The lively and cozy GARNI EDERA guesthouse is run by a family and is just a short stroll from the Borest ski slopes.

MID-RANGE

MOUNTAIN HOTEL MEZDï: Located in a serene Colfosco valley, this chalet epitomizes the alpine experience, including classic timber craftsmanship, charming planter boxes filled with lovely flowers, and breathtaking views of the mountains from the floor to ceiling windows.

HOTEL LAGO DI BRAIES: The three-star stone chalet hotel is situated directly on the shores of the most well-known lake in the Dolomites. It may be a little antiquated in certain areas, but since you're probably here for the lake, you probably don't want to spend a lot of time indoors anyway.

LUXURY

ROSA ALPINA: Built in 1850, this lovely family-run hotel exudes an old-world elegance while paying homage to Ladin customs with wood detailing, antiques from the area, and exquisite wall paintings. Additionally, St. Hubertus, the two-star restaurant, is located there.

ADLER MOUNTAIN LODGE: Perched atop the breathtaking Alpe di Siusi, this opulent and airy hotel offers panoramic views so breathtaking they seem straight out of a film.

(Best Restaurants) What And Where To Eat

We may be modest, but we'll own it: if Italy is considered one of the culinary royalties of the world, South Tyrol must be the jewel in its crown. Not only is South Tyrol the most Michelin-starred culinary region in the nation (19 restaurants share its 26 Michelin stars), but its cuisine combines centuries-old culinary traditions with the finest Italian cuisine and the hearty alpine influences of Austria and Germany to create utterly unique, scrumptiously delicious dishes that uplift the spirit.

Fresh pasta, locally produced cheese, the freshest ingredients, and hearty alpine meals that relieve sore muscles after a strenuous day in the great outdoors are all on the menu—of course, paired with excellent local wine! Good food is available almost everywhere in the area because most hotels and alpine lodges take great pride in the caliber of their chefs and restaurants.

We highly recommend trying these foods when you visit:

Knödel (dumplings): A combination of bread and regional cheese. They're quite tasty and filling.

Schlutzkrapfen: These ravioli-style dumplings with spinach, ricotta, and chives are far better than their name suggests.

Kaiserschmarrn: A light, shredded pancake eaten with applesauce and cream; an absolute dessert heaven.

Additionally, the following are a few must-visit eateries in the Dolomites:

Alpinn: Offering some of the best views of Kronplatz while serving produce that is produced locally. A local mountain-to-plate mentality informs Alpinn's delicious specialty risotto, which features wood sorrel and wild garlic. A Mountain Spritz created only with ingredients from the area is a must-have!

Oberholz: Housed in a creatively constructed alpine chalet, Oberholz serves insanely delicious risotto made with fresh mountain flowers and mushrooms.

Rifugio Ütia Bioch : With a view of Marmalada and situated on Piz Sorega, Rifugio Utia Bioch provides delicious South Tyrolean cuisine.

How Much Does It Cost To Visit The Dolomites?

The Dolomites aren't a cheap place to visit, but it's still less expensive than a trip to Switzerland. A road trip through the Dolomites will cost you between $100 and $150 USD per day for a rental car, $20 for parking, $150 to $200 USD per day for a double room in a 3-star hotel, $30 to $60 USD per person per day for food, and additional fees for cable cars (which vary). Although renting a car is a significant expenditure, it offers you greater mobility across the Dolomites and can save you time—which is quite valuable, particularly if you're visiting the area quickly. Budget travelers can save a lot of money by taking the bus or hiking from hut to hut; both are excellent options for seeing the Dolomites.

TRAVEL AND PACKING ESSENTIALS

You can experience a great deal of variety in this large country, from charming towns to seaside villages and contemporary metropolises. Selecting your travel attire is the next step after deciding on your dream vacation in Italy. After purchasing your tickets, reserving your lodging, and researching tours, you begin to dread the real task of packing your bags as the departure date draws near. I understand that packing for Italy—or any other destination—can always be a little difficult. This packing list for Italy includes everything you might need, so it doesn't matter if you're traveling there in the summer or the winter!

What To Pack For Your Trip

These practical add-ons will make your packing for Italy more comfortable. They're made to simplify your life and get you ready for everything that may come up on your journey.

Stainless Steel Bottle for Water

When I go on a trip, I always make sure to include my reusable water bottle. You'll not only reduce your usage of single-use plastic and save money, but you'll also save time by not having to stop and look for places that sell water bottles on a regular basis. Stainless steel water bottles use insulated technology to maintain the ideal temperature of your beverages, whether it be hot or cold. Your packing list for Italy should include this so you can stay hydrated at all times! In Italy, tap water is generally safe to drink, so you can just replenish it everywhere you go. Simply be cautious when requesting that bars or restaurants refill it for you, as this isn't as prevalent in Italy as it is in other parts of the world.

Stick & Tripod for Selfies

Italy is renowned for its breathtaking landscapes and captivating architecture, which make for the ideal photo backdrops. Keep a tripod and selfie stick close at hand to ensure you're always ready for photos. There will be photo ops wherever you look, and you won't have to bother approaching people to take your picture all the time.

Money Belt

Money Belt Pickpocketing is a widespread occurrence in tourist-heavy Italy, particularly in the larger cities. With an RFID money belt, your cash will be hidden, reducing the likelihood that it will be stolen. In contrast to the fanny pack, a money belt won't look bad with your attire. This travel accessory is virtually invisible because it may be worn under your shirt. Given its style and compact size, it won't detract from any of your amazing Italian ensembles.

Portable charger

Nobody enjoys getting a mobile phone notification about low battery life. You won't have to worry as much about preserving battery life if you have a portable charger. Having a cell phone is essential when traveling, not just for taking pictures but also for using Google Maps to make sure you're headed in the right direction or simply to look up information about the places you want to see. When traveling, this modest and easy addition to your Italy travel checklist will become your closest friend!

International adapter

To charge your electronics, you might require an adaptor depending on your point of origin. Instead of needing to purchase a new adaptor in each country I visit, I prefer to bring an international adapter with me wherever I go. Though they cost a little more and are somewhat thicker than those that simply have one kind of adaptor, they are ultimately worthwhile.

What To Pack: Clothing Essentials

Italy experiences seasonal variations in temperature. The four seasons are often harsher in northern Italy, whereas the south experiences slightly warmer weather. I'll leave it to you to figure out exactly what kind and quantity of socks and underwear to bring; nevertheless, I wanted to include a list of other clothing things that you would not typically consider but that will come in rather handy while visiting Italy. These must-have Italian outfits are ideal for every weather, whether you're trying to decide what to wear in the summer or the winter.

Shawl

A stylish scarf or wrap has multiple uses and is an excellent addition to any outfit. Italy is a nation that values traditions while still being quite fashion-conscious. You typically have to cover your shoulders and legs when you enter an Italian church. This need is easily met by a lightweight shawl. During the summer, when you're out exploring in the intense Italian sun, a shawl will shield you from the sun. It doubles as a scarf in the winter and adds another layer of warmth. Packing for Italy should include this versatile piece of apparel.

Stylish and Comfy Shoes

Striking a balance between comfort and style is a solid guideline for figuring out how to dress in Italy.

Travel purse or bag

You'll need somewhere to store all of your essential travel items when you're out and about in Italy for the entire day. Women can benefit greatly from anti-theft messenger bags, and men can accomplish the same goal with anti-theft shoulder backpacks. Specifically made travel bags and purses are your best bet. They feature numerous compartments to keep your belongings safe and secure, and they zip your goods away securely.

Polarized eyewear

A must-have item when deciding what to pack for Italy is polarized sunglasses. Today's top sunglasses feature lenses that have been polarized. These unique glasses lessen glare on snow, water, and roadways while blocking damaging UV rays. They are the excellent accompaniment for outdoor activities and suitable in all weather conditions. You will also be looking up a lot because of how large the buildings are in Italy. Your eyes will thank you later if you bring along a good pair of sunglasses.

Trendy Tops

Given that Italy is known for its fashion, a women's lookbook blouse is an excellent piece of apparel for women to bring along. You may accessorize it with jewelry and heels at night or tone it down with jeans and flats during the day. For men, remember to always keep it sleek and classy. A classy, timeless button-down shirt is always in vogue. A button-down shirt for guys is a fantastic choice. Wearing fashionable tops will help you fit in with Italian every day fashion.

Important Tips For Packing For A Vacation in Italy

Here are some crucial pointers I've learned throughout the years:

Wear loose clothing. If your jeans are too tight or your feet are painful and blistered, you won't enjoy your trip. Crucial: The most important thing I can advise you to do while packing for Italy is to have appropriate footwear that fits well.

Bring athletic sneakers if that's how you feel most comfortable wearing them; your feet will appreciate it.

Don't worry about "fitting in." You are not Italian, as every Italian you see knows it.

Accept a bit of the bella figura idea. The phrase "torne bella figura" refers to carrying yourself and your appearance well. If you wish to practice it, dress in clean, well-fitting, tailored, non-sporty attire—no yoga pants or XXL t-shirts for ladies or men. But I want you to know that it's also okay if you choose not to go with this style at all!

The same clothes can be worn over and again. If you wear the same shoes every day or the same outfit you wore the day before, nobody will notice (or care) as much as you think. Priotize enjoying your trip to the fullest.

Let go of the things you kept for "just in case." True, you may wish you had brought an additional sweater in October if the weather turns cold. What do you think? Should that actually happen, you can just purchase one in Italy- a wonderful justification for a shopping trip. Additionally, your Italian sweater will serve as a wonderful memento from your trip to Italy—one that you'll truly use.

Pack basic toiletries. While shopping in Italy can be enjoyable, it's best not to spend too much time looking for necessities. Basic toiletries are available in pharmacies, grocery stores, toiletry shops, and perfume shops in Italy, should you require them. Important Information: Make sure you bring everything you'll need for your first night and morning, including toothpaste, if you're coming in the evening when stores are closed.

Bring worn-in shoes along. It's never enjoyable to have blisters and uncomfortable shoes, especially if you intend to spend the entire day exploring Pompeii or Rome on foot. Similarly, make sure that before you come, you have put on your clothes. When you're traveling, itchy sweaters and slacks that ride up your butt are especially bothersome.

Select a simple/ muted color scheme. I advise staying with basic hues with pops of color or patterns, or neutrals (blacks, greys, whites, blue, browns, or creams). Don't forget about your propensity to spill. If you're a bit messy, stay away from wearing white since it will highlight the pasta stains from your mouthwatering Bologna tagliatelle al ragù.

Select fabric that would be great for travel. Select pieces that are easily and readily layered and allow for ventilation. In the event that you plan to do laundry on your travel, ensure that you carry clothes that can dry fast. Though many recommend linen for beach vacations in Italy, the fabric creases and stretches quickly, making it a poor choice for a travel "bring-along". It's true that Italians wear it, but they wash it before using it again.

Put underwear in your checked luggage. A backup pair of underwear, along with socks and a shirt, is now a must-have item in my carry-on luggage due to numerous delayed flights and lengthy layovers. If your bags get lost someplace, you'll be happy you have an extra pair.

Bring your favorite clothes and accessories. While talking about what to carry on vacation to Italy, I frequently hear comments like "don't pack that" or "you must leave that at home." It's crucial to carry items that you enjoy and that lift your mood. Bring your hair straightener, for instance, if feeling wonderful about your perfectly styled hair makes you feel amazing! (But, make sure the voltage is correct; a power converter could be required.)

Extra is less. When it comes to preparing for your first vacation to Italy, it entails filling your luggage up to halfway and then taking it down. If you have traveled to Italy before, you most likely have memories of packing too much for your initial visit. Remember that when you prepare for your next vacation!

Remain true to who you are. If you enjoy dressing up, you won't be happy trying to fit and travel with only five pieces of clothes into a carry-on suitcase for your month-long vacation to Italy. Bring your cosmetics if you like to apply a full face of makeup every day! If wearing leggings, a t-shirt, and a Patagonia fleece is how you feel most at ease, then go ahead and wear that outfit in Italy. While visiting lovely Italia, the most important thing is to be at ease and content.

THE-ALL-YOU-NEED-TO-KNOW-GUIDE FOR PLANNING THE PERFECT NORTHERN ITALY TRAVEL ITINERARY

You're considering taking a trip to Northern Italy, but you're not sure where to go or how long to stay. Discover the ideal Northern Italy itinerary with the help of this guide, which includes Venice's palazzos, chic Milan, vibrant fishing villages, breathtaking Alpine views, lovely lakes, and slopes covered in vineyards. Awaiting the journey of a lifetime?

Among the most traveled nations in Europe, if not the entire globe, is Italy. Among the main draws are the exquisite food, immaculate beaches, elaborate cathedrals, and ancient ruins. There are 20 regions in Il Bel Paese, and each one is more tempting than the last. Northern Italy offers a combination of quaint little villages and busy tourist destinations.

Venice is without a doubt the jewel in the crown of northern Italy, but the Cinque Terre, Milan, the lake district, and of course the breathtaking Dolomites region also have a lot to offer. This travel guide to Northern Italy walks you through the must-see places in the area, recommend places to eat, show you how to get around, and includes an example schedule for a one- or two-week vacation.

How Long Should My Itinerary For Northern Italy Be?

Northern Italy offers so much to see and do that a person might easily spend a month exploring it all. Unfortunately, though, most of us can only dream of unending vacations. You can witness a small portion of what's available in a week.

A WEEK: If your schedule is jam-packed with stops like Milan, the Dolomites, and Venice, you'll need to rent a car to get about more quickly.

TWO WEEKS: This amount of time allows for a little more breathing room and guarantees that exploring Cinque Terre and the stunning Lake Garda may be included in the schedule without feeling overly hurried. In this situation, you could choose to move slowly and get around using the public transportation system to get to the different locations.

Best Time To Visit Northern Italy?

Any time of year is an excellent time for a holiday in Northern Italy, though it really depends on your interests. The average winter temperature in Milan is 5°C, or 45°F. Northern Italy experiences chilly winters, and many popular tourist destinations have much quieter winter hours with seasonal pubs & restaurants closed from December to March.

By the end of March and the beginning of April, temperatures begin to rise, and they continue to do so until the end of October (18°C/65°F). To avoid the crowds and to experience Northern Italy tourism at its best, choose the shoulder seasons of April through June and September through October. This will give you plenty of time for dolce far niente in small towns and villages. The first snowfall in the Dolomites typically occurs in October. If the mere mention of snow makes you tremble instantly—as it does for me—avoid traveling to Northern Italy after September.

How To Get Around / Navigate Northern Italy?

When it comes to public transportation, Northern Italy is the most developed region of the country. All of the cities in Northern Italy can be easily reached by regional trains and buses. Smaller communities may be more difficult and time-consuming to reach, particularly in the rocky Dolomites; consequently, if you're pressed for time and have a Northern Italy schedule, you might want to consider hiring a car.

It is possible to check into hiring an electric car if you do decide to rent a car because Northern Italy has a lot of electric car charging stations. As an alternative, consider making reservations at a green hotel with a charging station in the Dolomites.

Car rental in Italy

An excellent idea would be to rent a car and take a road trip around Northern Italy! It offers you the greatest freedom and command over your own timetable. It should come as no surprise that there will be some driving involved, just to give you an idea. It is around 340 kilometers (211 miles) from

Vernazza (Cinque Terre) to Venice, traveling through the high Dolomites region.

The community respects road signs and red lights, and the roads are kept up nicely. Respect that diminishes as you go south in Italy. The price per day for renting a car in Northern Italy ranges from €30 to €80 ($32 to $85), depending on the type of vehicle and insurance you choose.

Budget Advice: Make sure to reserve in early and compare rentals with Auto Europe!

Required Paperwork For A Car Rental In Northern Italy

AGE: The minimum age requirement for drivers is 19. Drivers between the ages of 19 and 25 must be aware that there will be an additional fee (young driver surcharge).

A LICENSE TO DRIVE: A current driver's license. If you are renting from a location outside of Europe, you must have an international driver's license.

INSURANCE: It is mandatory by Italian law to have theft protection and collision damage waiver insurance for your vehicle. It's wise to verify ahead of time, but these are typically included in the basic rental package!

Northern Italy's Public Transportation System

TRAIN:

Trains, both national and regional, wind their way through the several cities of Northern Italy. They will take you from Milan to Venice, stopping frequently at small towns along the way. It is simple to travel by train in Italy, but you will need to exercise some patience because the trains are often delayed. Obtain your passes: Create your schedule and buy tickets on Omio.

BUS:

Because every region has its own bus company, rides between them can be a little more complicated. It proved to be a little difficult to obtain the most recent schedule. I was only able to successfully take the bus in the South Tyrol and Trentino province (Dolomites), and even then, it was just to get from one place inside the same region to another.

TIP: Look into the Mobil Card for South Tyrol and the Guest Pass for Trentino. You can use the cards to get on the bulk of public transportation in the area; they can only be bought once.

Overview Of The Itinerary For Northern Italy

The amount of time you have available will largely determine where you go in the North of Italy. Saying that there is a lot to see and do is an understatement; it is not possible to fit it all into a single trip.

While the distances may not appear great, keep in mind that Northern Italy's Eastern and Western shores are separated by a massive mountain range. The stunning Piedmont region, which is recognized for its wine and breathtaking scenery, is not included in this guide.

GOING THERE: Take a plane into Venice Marco Polo Airport (VCE) and out of one of Milan's three international airports, Malpensa, Linate, and the neighboring Bergamo. Seek out the best deal using Skyscanner.

GETTING AROUND: If you are renting a car, return it to the airport in Milan when you arrive in Venice. To navigate Venice, a car is not necessary! Instead, put your money on some delectable Cicchetti! Verify rental prices with Auto Europe.

A One-Week Itinerary For Northern Italy

Day One and Day Two: Milan

It's evident as soon as you get off the train that Milan is the financial and fashion center of Italy. Superbly attired locals, many in black, flit in and out of luxury shops and fancy restaurants. Milan is the best destination in Northern Italy if you're searching for a wonderful place to go shopping or for a weekend getaway.

Must see locations in Milan:

- Milan is big—I promise—very, really big. The most recognizable method to navigate the city is by taking one of the numerous trams. A biglietto gionaliero (day ticket) costs €4.5 ($4.8) and may be purchased at the Metro station or any newsagent in the area. With this ticket, you can utilize the metro, buses, and trams all day long.

- There are many highlights in Milan; plan to spend two full days exploring the city's culinary, culture, and art. The world's oldest retail mall, the Galleria Vittorio Emanuele II, is a sight to behold. Starting with the classics, the 14th-century Duomo di Milano boasts a terrace with views to die for (cathedral + terrace tickets €20/ $17 ($21/$19) can be bought online).

- Visit the striking Castello Sforzescoa, an amazing 15th-century medieval stronghold, a kilometer's walk from the Duomo (entry costs €5 ($5.3)). The oldest structure in Milan, Sant Ambrogio, dates back to 379 AD and is a proud example of Milan's history. Admission is €2 ($2.10).

- The Last Supper by Leonardo da Vinci is on display in the Santa Marie delle Grazie Convent next, with entrance tickets costing €6 ($6.40). Caravaggio fans can view the artist's piece Supper at Emmaus at the Pinacoteca di Brera (entry tickets €15 ($16)). The famed "home of opera," La Scala, is unquestionably the cherry on top of the art sundae. Guided tours are available for €25 ($26.70), or you can choose to indulge and attend one of the many performances.)

- Head over to the Darsena district for dinner and a well-earned aperitivo.

Accommodations in Milan

BEST VIEWS: Amabilia Suites

A hotel room view of the Duomo is difficult to top. It doesn't get much more central than this: the hotel is situated 300 yards (328 yards) from Palazzo Reale and 100 yards (109 yards) from Duomo Square!

THE MOST BANG FOR YOUR BUCK: Biocities

Situated close to both downtown Milan and the Milano Central Train Station, both at walking distance. On its premises, the Biocity hotel exclusively employs environmentally friendly products. Making use of a certified zero-emission climate control system and serving organic pastries for breakfast.

Day Three–Day Five: Dolomites

Spend days three, four, and five of your seven-day journey to Northern Italy in the Dolomites.

Sud Tirol, the northernmost part of Italy, is perched on the Italian side of the Dolomites Alps and is essentially a continuation of Austria, to which it borders. Since you only have a week to spend in Northern Italy, this is the area of the Dolomites that I recommend you see!

Beyond just their physical proximity, the two locations are linked by culture and language: Sud Tirol's vibe is in fact closer to that of Innsbruck or Munich than it is to the nearby regions of Italy, and despite being officially bilingual, the region is primarily an autonomous German-speaking region where Italian is frequently only spoken as a second language by its residents.

Must see locations in the Dolomites:

Bolzano

Discover the Dolomites in Bolzano, the capital of Sud Tirol, a charming city with a long history as a commercial center. The city's structures and several squares, where city markets are held today just way they were in the Middle Ages, are still striking examples of this legacy. It is possible to spend a few hours exploring the city and taking in its principal attractions, which include Walther Square, the 15th-century Cathedral, and Castle Maretsch.

A note for the mountaineer enthusiast: For those with an intense interest in mountaineering, Bolzano is home to Reinhold Messner's Messner Mountain Museum.

Lake Geneva/Kaisersee

Bolzano is the ideal starting point for the Lago di Carezza/Kaersee, which is just a 30-minute scenic drive from South Tyrol's city. Northern Italy is renowned for its abundance of stunning lakes. With its glistening green water, evergreen trees encircling it, and the Dolomites providing a picturesque backdrop, the lake is a modest but perfectly formed example of a classic alpine lake in the Dolomites.

The Tré Cime and Val Pusteria

Proceed eastward from Bolzano in the direction of Val Pusteria. Drive via the stunning Alpi di Siusi, Europe's largest alpine highland, en route. They have endless miles of trails and mountain paths to offer, suitable for both the inexperienced and the most experienced climbers.

A careful eye will pick up on the numerous vineyards scattered over the area. The South Tyrol's Wine Route, which runs between Nalles in the north and Salorno in the south, is a breathtaking section of road lined with vineyards growing the grapes used to make the region's well-known white wines. Don't miss it.

After arriving in Val Pusteria, you should think about spending the night in San Candido (we stayed at the Leitlhof Hotel), which is ideally situated between the most well-known attractions in Northern Italy, including the renowned Tre Cime di Lavaredo, Lago di Braies, and Lago di Dobbiaco. There are not enough words to express how beautiful this area is.

What to Eat/ Drink in the Dolomites

Let's face it: Since you are organizing a trip to Northern Italy, you are probably already daydreaming about the cuisine and wine you will enjoy there. The Dolomites' traditional food is an intriguing fusion of Italian, Swiss, and Austrian cuisines.

Known for its abundance of meat, potatoes, and cheese, some of its most well-known dishes are the Austrian-inspired Strudel and Kaiserschmarrn (fluffy shredded pancake with jam), Ravioli alla Pusterese/Schlutzkrapfen (stuffed pasta made from rye and wheat flour), and Canederli (boiled dumplings, traditionally done with the available leftovers).

A Note for Driving in the Dolomites

You must be ready for the millions of "Tornanti"—hairpin bends—if you have decided to take a road trip to see the best of Northern Italy. It might not be a terrible idea to get in the front seat, or better yet, behind the wheel, if you suffer from carsickness like I do. Fortunately, the roads are kept up nicely, and drivers honor the traffic laws, albeit to a greater extent than in the southern region of Italy.

The majority of the time, parking is reasonably priced and conveniently accessible (i.e., just a short stroll from the destination). However, during peak tourist seasons, many of the most well-known attractions, including Lago di Braies, have their main roadways closed from around 9 to around 5 in order to lessen traffic and pollution.

Day Six and Seven: Venice

Venice is a Northern Italian must-see that rarely needs an introduction. During the Middle Ages and Renaissance, it was a great financial and nautical power, a staging point for the Crusades, and a vital hub of commerce. It served as the capital of the Republic of Venice for more than a millennium.

Venice, which has managed to retain much of its former splendor, is the capital of the Veneto region and a must-see destination on any tour through Northern Italy. Constructed atop 118 islands and linked by more than 400 bridges, Venice provides its countless visitors a scene that no other city can match, replete with winding lanes, imposing Palazzi, and more churches than one could possibly explore in a single week.

Accommodation Advice: Book a room in Cannaregio, the more quaint and residential area of Venice. Not far from the mouthwatering street food and far from the throngs of visitors! We stayed at the gorgeous Grand Hotel Palazzo Dei Dogi, which was slightly pricey but well worth it for the excellent breakfast and service.

Must see locations in Venice:

Discover Venice's Many Neighborhoods.

Knowing Venice's topography is essential before embarking on an exploration of the city. The six sestieri (neighborhoods) that make up Venice proper are San Marco and have the most beautiful architecture. But this precedence is followed by another: The San Marco district becomes tremendously busy as the great bulk of people visiting Venice swarm the area.

Cannaregio, the largest and most northern neighborhood of Venice, is my favorite. It is brimming with bars serving the well-known Cicchetti (tapas) of Venice and serves as the ideal pied-à-terre for touring the rest of the city or indulging in a delectable aperitivo. Remarkably, Cannaregio is also the location of Venice's ghetto, which is the first in the world, and its five synagogues, which are a must-see when visiting Venice.

See The Many Churches And Palaces In Venice.

Let's return, though, to the reason you traveled to Venice: the palaces and churches. Naturally, Piazza San Marco, the city's historical and modern center, comes first. Each and every trip to Venice revolves around the plaza, which is home to the Basilica di San Marco, the Clock Tower—the highest structure in the city—and the Palazzo Ducale, the headquarters of the Repubblica di Venezia government.

Built to dazzle foreign functionaries who would want to meet with Venice's greats, Palazzo Ducale is an architectural celebration of the city's grandeur that still astounds museum visitors today.

Part of it, and open to visitors of the Palazzo, is the well-known Bridge of Sighs, renowned for its exquisite architecture. The inmate traversing it to get to the prisons across the canal, which is why the Bridges got their name, must not have thought it was as lovely.

The Rialto Bridge, the Ponte dell'Accademia, the Grand Canal, and the Peggy Guggenheim Collection—which is home to some of the most exquisite pieces of 20th-century American and European art—are additional must-see attractions in Venice.

Save Time: Purchase your tickets early to avoid the often lengthy and often brutal lineup at Dodge Palace and St. Mark's Basillica (which offers terrace access), especially during the sweltering summer months. Purchase tickets online.

Explore Burano and Murano.

I advise you to include Murano and Burano on your list of things to see in Venice if you want to take a vacation from the city. Situated about ten minutes by boat from Venice, the former is the home of renowned glassblowers who skillfully craft amazing artwork by infusing air into heated glass.

HOW TO GO THERE: Take a boat to Torcello Island, Burano, and Murano. Organize a guided day tour, or just reserve your transportation and spend a half-day exploring the islands.

Where in Venice to Stay

RECOMMENDED STAY: Grand Hotel Palazzo Dei Dogi

Situated in the quiet district of Cannaregio, this opulent hotel offers a peaceful haven. housed in a magnificently remodeled palace with the city's largest private garden.

THE BEST VIEWS: Palazzo Da Ponte 03 (Airbnb)

Not just any Airbnb, but one right in the middle of Venice with an amazing view over the canals. The hotel-quality linens and immaculate rooms are provided, and our host's advice was quite helpful.

Venice Food and Drink Recommendations

For a list of available restaurants, view our chapter which includes restaurant addresses and contact details. A guide on Venice's food would be remiss in its duty if it did not begin with a mention of Aperol Spritz. Although this cocktail has been around since the early 19th century, the Barbieri brothers in nearby Pauda ultimately developed it into its current shape in 1919. Not only is the Aperol Spritz a local favorite these days, it's also a globally recognized beverage that's available everywhere, but nowhere is it as good—or as affordable—as Venice.

In relation to that, are you trying to find inexpensive and filling food in Venice to go with your spritz? The word "cicchetti" is most frequently used to describe the antipasti, or Venetian tapas, tradition, which is served as a tiny plate (tapas) or finger food during happy hour (aperitivo). Cicchetti is inexpensive and typically served with an ombra, or small round glass of wine, such as an Aperol Spritz.

Bacari bars in Venice serve a variety of tiny dishes, nibbles, and bite-sized snacks. A few of the more popular Cicchetti meals in Venice are buranelli biscuits for a sweeter flavor, fritto misto di mare (a mixture of fried seafood), baccalà mantecato, and sarde in saor.

Venice Parking

You may be shocked to learn that since Venice is a lagoon, cars are not permitted within unless they can also be used as boats! As a result, I advise you to give up your rental car and proceed with your trip across Northern Italy without a vehicle. In case you choose to retain your rental vehicle, you can park it at Tronchetto Parking (€21 ($21) per night).

How To Go From The Tronchetto Parking To Venice

The People Mover, a small electric railway, connects this parking lot to the heart of Venice proper. It costs €1.5 ($1.60) and takes you to Piazzale Roma, from where you may catch a Vaporetto (€7.5 ($8) every 75 minutes) to explore the various areas of the lagoon.

Itinerary For An Additional Week In Northern Italy (Two-Week Travel)

Two weeks in Northern Italy should be spent visiting the Cinque Terre, Milan, Lake Garda, Dolomites, Venice, and perhaps a pit break. Venice

GOING THERE: Since you have chosen to stay in Northern Italy for 14 days, there are countless ways to extend the suggested 7-day schedule! Flying into Pisa International Airport (PSA) and out of Venice Marco Polo Airport (VCE) is what I would personally advise. Seek out the best deal using Skyscanner.

GETTING AROUND: If you are hiring a car, picking it up in Milan will be the least expensive alternative. To go around Cinque Terre, you won't require a car. Once you arrive in Venice, leave the car behind and take a direct train (one hour's travel) to Verona. Verify rental prices with Auto Europe.

Days One to Three: Cinque Terre

The Cinque Terre, or more specifically the five charming villages that make up the Cinque Terre National Park—Rimaggiore, Manarola, Corniglia, Vernazza, and Monterosso al Mare—are among the most popular tourist destinations in Northern Italy. For travelers who love taking pictures, these pastel-colored settlements perched on cliffs and encircled by breathtaking turquoise waters are a genuine paradise.

Since the little towns are manageable and can be explored in a half day, visiting two of them in one day is totally doable without feeling rushed. Traveling by train from one town to another (no vehicles allowed). Every day, trains depart every 30 minutes.

Where of stay: Stay at Monterosso al Mare; it has plenty of busy pubs and restaurants and the best train connections to Milan. La Serra Sul Mare (those vistas!), Villa Tanca (beachfront), and Agriturismo Buranco (recommended) are a few fantastic local and sustainable guesthouses.

Must see locations in Cinque Terre:

Riomaggiore

Most visitors to the Cinque Terre stay at Riomaggiore, which is the village closest to La Spezia. The charming village's pastel-colored homes and stunning beach fringed with cliffs are somewhat reminiscent of Rovinj in Croatia.

Some of the highlights are sunning on the pebble beach Spiaggia di Riomaggiore, hiking the Sanctuary of Montenero for 3.5 km in a circle, leisurely strolling along Via Colombo in the old town, and watching the sun set over the port (sunset site may be located here).

Tip: Take advantage of the Cinque Terre Ferry, which connects the different settlements via water and costs €27 ($29) per day. Get your tickets at the main ticket office on the day of the event.

Manarola

Manarola, a popular destination for tourists, is charming with its pastel perfection and rocky beaches. During golden hour, the Manarola Scenic Viewpoint (found here) is a must-visit location for both professional and amateur photographers. Stroll through Via Renato Birolli and Via Antonio Discovolo, popping in and out of independent shops brimming with handcrafted trinkets. Enjoy a pizza at the waterfront while watching the sun set over the ocean to round off the day. It may seem corny, but it's well worth it.

Corniglia

In contrast to the settlements around it, Corniglia is not situated directly on the beach. Rather, it is perched on a hilltop and offers breathtaking views in every direction. A stroll around the ancient town will amply demonstrate that point. The endless views and the serenity (fewer people visit Corniglia) are the key attractions here.

Vernazza

The small village of Vernazza is without a doubt one of the most breathtaking locations in all of Northern Italy. Numerous tourists have been motivated to visit the area by images of golden hour from the well-known viewpoint (located here). Swimming and tanning by the harbor, going to the Doria Castle, seeing the stunning Chiesa di Santa Margherita d'Antiochio, and trekking some of the blue trail are some of Vernazza's top attractions.

Monterosso al Mare

Out of the five villages, Monterosso al Mare is the most advanced. It features two distinct towns: the "old" town is magnificent in its pastel perfection, while the "new" town is home to numerous excellent restaurants and bars. See the Oratorio dei Neri, the church of the dead, the Fieschi castle, the Capuchin Monastery, and the church of Saint John the Baptist.

Getting to Cinque Terre from Pisa

Proceed to the Pisa Centrale train station after landing at Pisa International Airport; taking the PisaMover, a high-speed shuttle, will make the journey simple. It is a swift five-minute rail travel, with tickets costing €2.7 ($2.9). Get your tickets at the departure station directly.

Your next destination from the Pisa Centrale train station is Cinque Terre. There is no such place as a "Cinque Terre" train station; instead, look for trains that travel to Riomaggiore, Manarola, Corniglia, Vernazza, and Monterosso al Mare, the five villages that make up the Cinque Terre National Park. You will need to change trains in La Spezia in order to reach the majority of these communities.

Obtain your passes: Use Omio to check train schedules and buy tickets online.

Days Five to Six: Lago Di Garda

Città di Castello travel the rail to Milan and stay there for two days. On days six and seven of your two-week vacation in Northern Italy, drive from Milan towards Lago di Garda and explore the lake.

It would be like going to Belgium and without eating chocolate to find a Northern Italy itinerary that does not include at least one of the lakes in the well-known Italian lake. That's right—just not done! The five stunning lakes of Lake Maggiore, Lugano, Como, Isea, and Garda are located in the Italian Lake District.

Part of Lago di Garda is situated in the province of Trentino, one of the three provinces that comprise the Dolomites region. After renting a car in Milan, head 168 kilometers (104 miles) or 2 hours and 22 minutes to Riva del Garda, which will serve as your base of operations for the next two days of sightseeing.

Budget tip: On a tight budget, consider the Garda Guest Card, which offers a range of savings on tickets for public transit around the lake and discounts on other activities.

Activities To Do at Lake Garda

The largest lake in Italy is Lake Garda, which covers an area of 370 square kilometers (143 square miles). The immaculate lake, encircled by craggy mountain peaks that plunge into azure waters, provides a much-needed respite from Milan's congestion. Discovering the picture-perfect villages tucked away on the banks of the make is all that's required.

There are various activities available for the energetic visitor, such as hiking the well-known GardaTrek, which consists of three routes with different durations and levels of difficulty, riding around the lake on designated bike paths, or leisurely strolling around the several towns. To name a few, there is Sirmione, Riva del Garda, Desenzano del Garda, and Limone sul Garda.

Where to stay around Lake Garda

SUGGESTED: The Eco Hotel Ariston

This family-run hotel boasts a breathtaking view of the Scaligeri Castle, some of the oldest waterfront buildings in the town, and Lake Garda. It's perfectly situated close to the ancient town center and a couple trailheads.

VALUE FOR MONEY: Hotel Zanella epOche

Remain in a stunning, yet reasonably priced, three-star hotel on Lake Garda that has its own private beach. This family-owned hotel provides a culinary experience using only organic ingredients.

Day Seven: Verona

On your final day in Northern Italy, go out and spend a day exploring Verona. Just 120 kilometers (75 miles) separate Venice and Verona, making it a perfect day travel destination. Even though it is not as charming as Venice or Florence, it nonetheless has a charming arena that can rival the Colosseum in magnificence! Plan a day excursion to Verona if you have time to spare when traveling through Northern Italy.

Trains go between Venice (Stazione di Venezia Santa Lucia) and Verona (Verona Porta Nuova) several times every day.

Comfortable 1 hour 30 minute train travel; tickets start at €9 ($9.6).

Activities in Verona

For lovers, Verone is among the top destinations in Northern Italy. Though it was not originally planned, I ended up spending half a day in Verona, the medieval city that served as the backdrop for Shakespeare's Romeo and Julieette.

Getting lost in the numerous tiny lanes of the Centro Storico—the first-century Verona Arena being the ultimate highlight—was my favorite thing to do when visiting Verona. Unfortunately, it was closed when we went, but I've heard that it still has a lot of concerts, especially in the summer. Prior to visiting, check their calendar or schedule a guided tour.

Just before it closes (18:30 PM), stop by Juliette's residence instead of the museum. Due to its 20th-century addition, the balcony is somewhat of a tourist trap, but it is still charming enough to warrant a quick, corny photo. Climb the Torre dei Lamberti (€6 ($6.4)) for a breathtaking view over Verona's terracotta roofs, and be sure to catch golden hour when crossing the Ponte Pietra.

Invest the evening in Verona: It's a wonderful day excursion from Venice. If you really wish to stay in the city longer, you might choose to reserve one night. The Verona Luxury

Apartments offer the greatest views, Hotel Colomba d'Oro is a luxurious indulgence, and B&B Tosca offers the best value for your money.

Itinerary For Northern Italy: Closing Thoughts

Though many people only associate Northern Italy with a visit to Venice or the Cinque Terre, the area has much more to offer. If you rent a car, two weeks is the ideal amount of time to stay in Northern Italy. Since there are plenty of charging stations in Northern Italy, you might want to rent or drive an electric vehicle while there.

Take a flight to Pisa, spend a few days in Cinque Terre's five picture-perfect villages or in pastel perfection; take the train to chic Milan and see the sights; rent a car and drive to Lago di Garda for hiking and swimming; then spend a few days exploring the breathtaking Dolomites Area.

Take a drive to the breathtaking city of Venice, return the rental car, and spend the next two days seeing this beautiful city in Northern Italy. Consume copious amounts of Aperol Spritz and fill up on plenty of Venetian street cuisine (ciccheti). Take the train to medieval Verona, the setting for Shakespeare's Romeo and Juliet, and spend the day exploring the city. And thus, Northern Italy was subjugated!

CONCLUSION + FREE TEN PAGES OF TRAVEL JOURNAL

Finally, my dear traveller, Northern Italy is an affair of the heart rather than merely a place to visit. It is the place where the timeless beauty of the land, the kindness of the people, and the symphony of flavors all combine to produce a tune that will never be forgotten.

You've become a part of a centuries-old tale as you've walked the charming alleys of Verona, tasted the delectable cuisine of Bologna, traveled back in time, and marveled at the medieval and renaissance architecture of Genoa. It's a tale of ardor, ancestry, and life's fundamental qualities.

That being said, Northern Italy has made its lasting impression on your spirit, whether you have strolled through the medieval streets of Milan or buried yourself in the serene embrace of Lake Garda. It is a place with beauty you've not only deeply felt but also seen and experienced.

Take home with you the memories of sun setting over the Dolomites, the taste of freshly made pasta, and the echo of laughter from Venetian piazzas. These recollections should serve as a reminder that Northern Italy is a region you never truly leave behind.

You have not merely visited Northern Italy; you have lived, loved, and integrated yourself into an enduring story. Thus, may your heart always beat to the beat of Italian life and may your spirit always yearn for the enchantment that is Northern Italy, till we meet again in this land of dreams. Farewell, my friend, and may the rest of your travels be just as amazing as the ones you've made thus far.

Made in the USA
Las Vegas, NV
24 January 2024